BASSOON BOOK 3

I0805396

ESSENTIAL TECHNIQUE
for Band

INTERMEDIATE TO ADVANCED STUDIES

TIM LAUTZENHEISER • JOHN HIGGINS • CHARLES MENGHINI
PAUL LAVENDER • TOM C. RHODES • DON BIERSCHENK

To create an account, visit:
www.essentialelementsinteractive.com

Student Activation Code
E3BN-1376-8528-3426

ISBN 979-835013667-8

HAL•LEONARD®
A Muse Group Company

B♭ MAJOR

1. SCALE AND ARPEGGIO

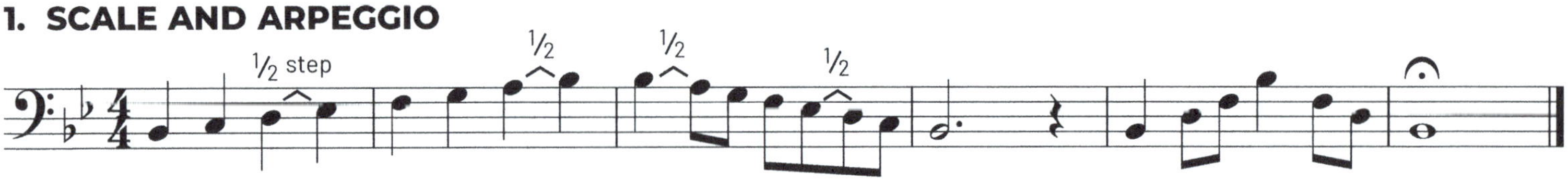

2. EXERCISE IN THIRDS

3. ARPEGGIO STUDY

4. TWO-PART ETUDE

5. CHROMATIC SCALE

6. BALANCE BUILDER

THEORY

divisi or *div.*	Divide the written parts among players, usually into two parts, with equal numbers playing each part.
unison or *a2*	All players play the same part (usually found after a *divisi* section).

7. CHORALE

8. GREAT GATE OF KIEV

Modeste Mussorgsky

9. CHILDREN'S SHOES

African American Spiritual

HISTORY

English composer **George Frideric Handel** (1685–1759) is among the best known composers of the **Baroque Period (1600–1750)**. *Sound an Alarm* (from *Judas Maccabaeus*) and his most famous work, the *Hallelujah Chorus* (from *Messiah*), are two well-known melodies from his **oratorios** – large scale works for solo voices, chorus, and orchestra.

10. SOUND AN ALARM

George Frideric Handel

11. HALLELUJAH CHORUS

George Frideric Handel

12. RHYTHM RAP *Clap the rhythm while counting and tapping.*

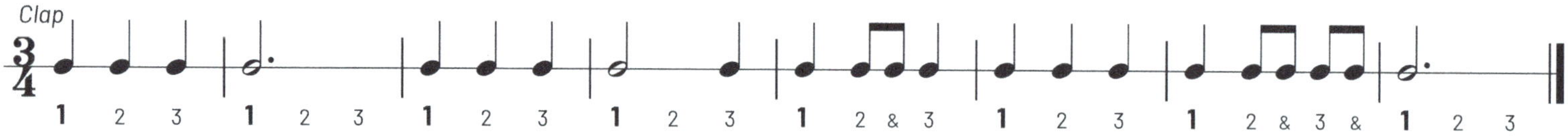

THEORY

3/8 Time Signature

= **3 beats** per measure
= **Eighth** note gets one beat

♪ = 1 beat ♩ = 2 beats ♩. = 3 beats

3/8 time is usually played with a slight emphasis on the 1st beat of each measure. In faster music, this primary beat will make the music feel like it's counted "in 1."

13. RHYTHM RAP *Compare this exercise with No. 12.*

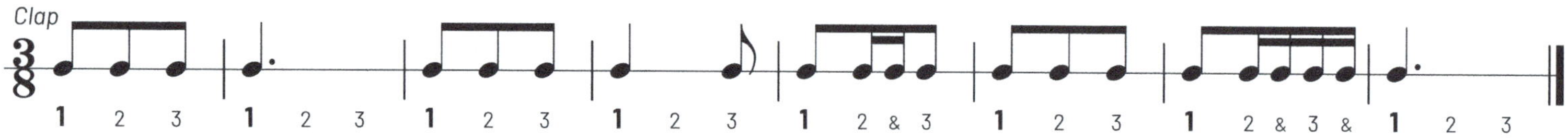

14. WALTZ PETITE

15. MOLLY BANN

English Folk Song

THEORY

9/8 Time Signature

= **9 beats** per measure
= **Eighth** note gets one beat

♪ = 1 beat ♩. = 3 beats
♩ = 2 beats 𝅗𝅥. = 6 beats

9/8 time is usually played with a slight emphasis on the **1st**, **4th**, and **7th** beats of each measure. This divides the measure into 3 groups of 3 beats each. In faster music, these three primary beats will make the music feel like it's counted "in 3."

16. RHYTHM RAP *Clap the rhythm while counting and tapping.*

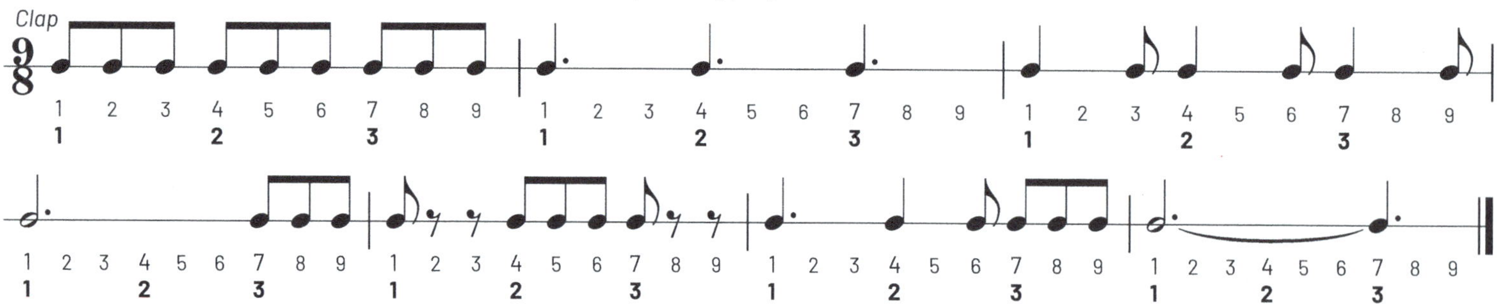

17. SUNDAY AT NINE

G MINOR

Minor Keys

Minor keys and their scales sound different from major keys because of their different pattern of whole and half steps. Each minor key is *relative* or "related" to the major key with the same key signature.

The simplest form of a minor key is called **natural minor**. Two other types are **harmonic minor** and **melodic minor**, each of which have certain altered tones.

18. NATURAL MINOR

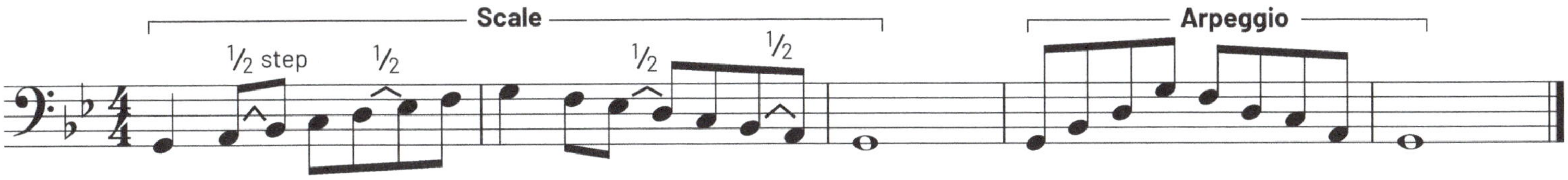

19. HARMONIC MINOR

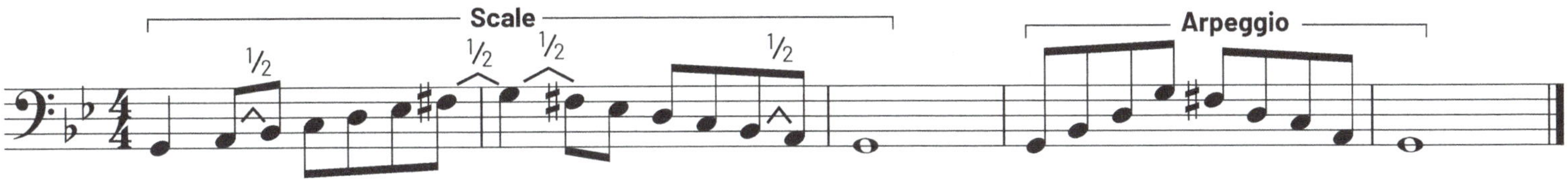

20. PAT-A-PAN

French

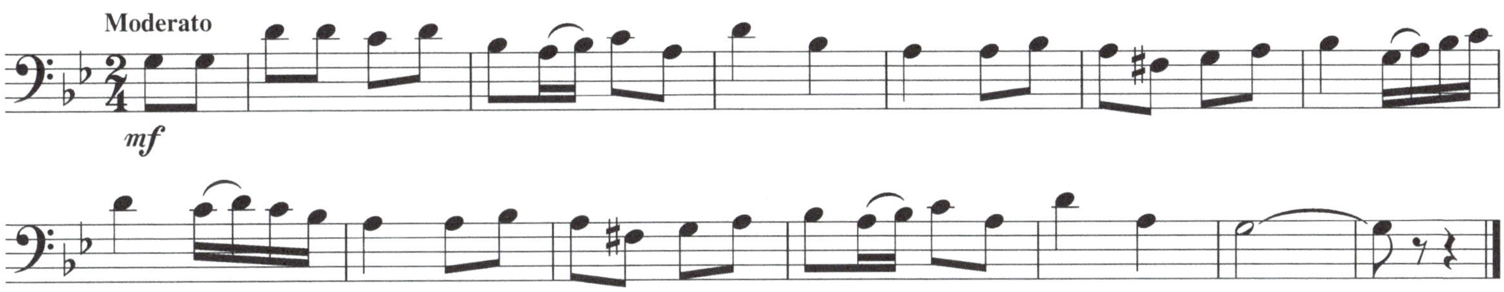

21. THE SLEDGEHAMMER SONG

Russian

22. ESSENTIAL ELEMENTS QUIZ – AUSTRALIAN FOLK SONG

Australian

E♭ MAJOR

23. SCALE AND ARPEGGIO *Practice both upper and lower octaves.*

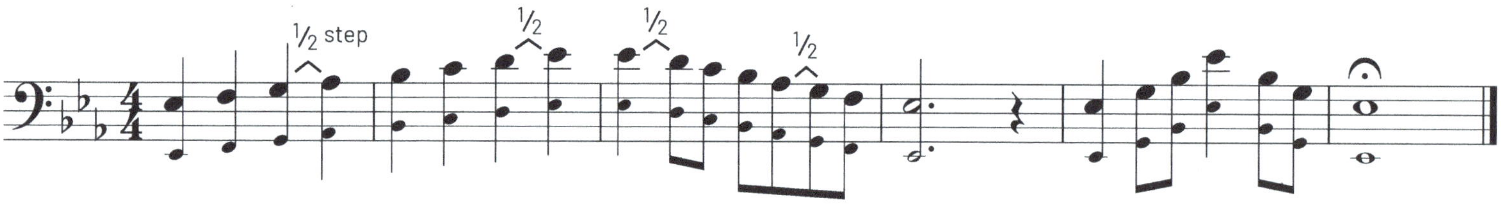

24. EXERCISE IN THIRDS

25. ARPEGGIO STUDY

26. TWO-PART ETUDE

27. CHROMATIC SCALE

28. BALANCE BUILDER

29. CHORALE

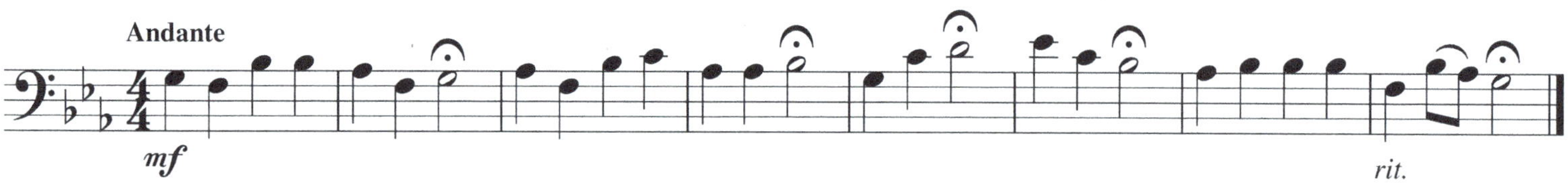

Austrian composer **Johann Strauss Jr.** (1825–1899) is also known as "The Waltz King." He wrote some of the world's most famous waltzes (dances in 3/4 meter). This waltz is from *Die Fledermaus* ("The Bat"), Strauss' most famous **operetta**. Operettas were the forerunners of today's musicals, such as *Oklahoma*, *The Sound of Music*, *The Phantom of the Opera*, *Wicked*, and *Hamilton*.

30. ADELE'S SONG

Johann Strauss Jr.

31. MARINE'S HYMN

32. RHYTHM RAP

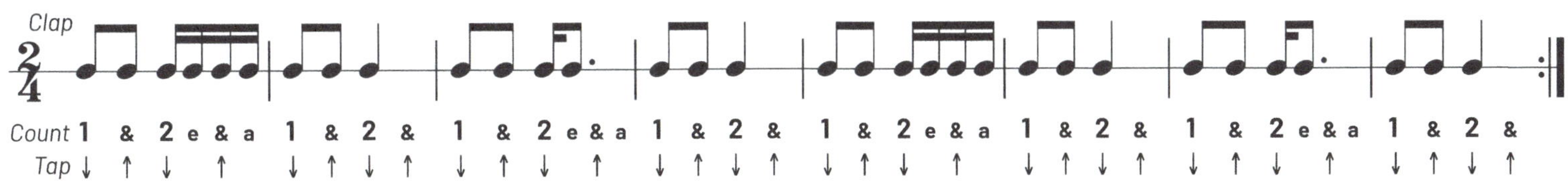

33. KEEPIN' SECRETS

Appalachian Folk Song

34. THE KEEL ROW

Sea Song

35. JACK'S THE MAN

THEORY

12/8 Time Signature

12/8 = **12 beats** per measure
= **Eighth** note gets one beat

♪ = 1 beat
♩ = 2 beats
♩. = 3 beats
𝅗𝅥. = 6 beats
𝅗𝅥.‿♩. = 9 beats
𝅝. = 12 beats

12/8 time is usually played with a slight emphasis on the **1st**, **4th**, **7th**, and **10th** beats of each measure. This divides the measure into 4 groups of 3 beats each. These four primary beats will make the music feel like it's counted "in 4."

36. RHYTHM RAP *Clap the rhythm while counting and tapping.*

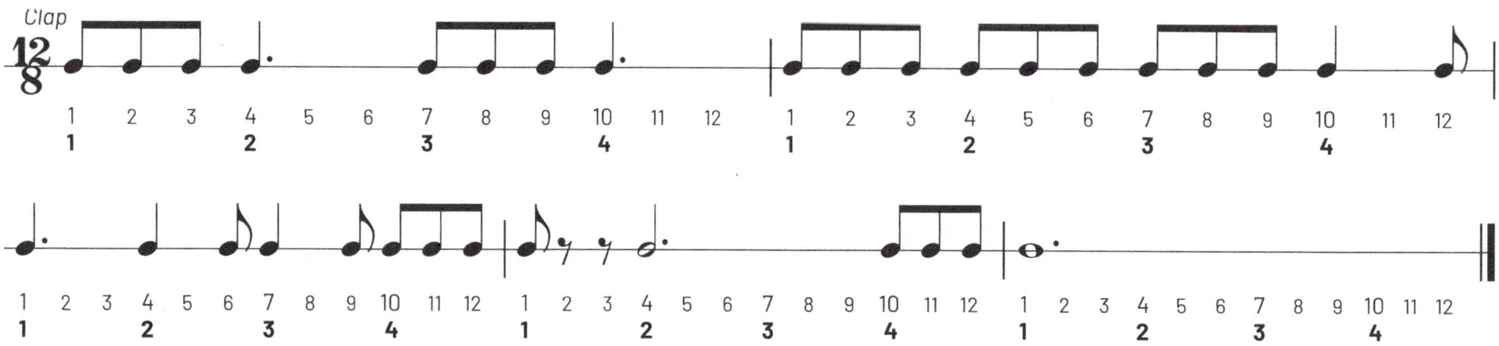

37. SERENADE

38. WITH THINE EYES

Lento ◄ *Slowly*

▲ *molto = "much"*

C MINOR

39. NATURAL MINOR *Practice both upper and lower octaves.*

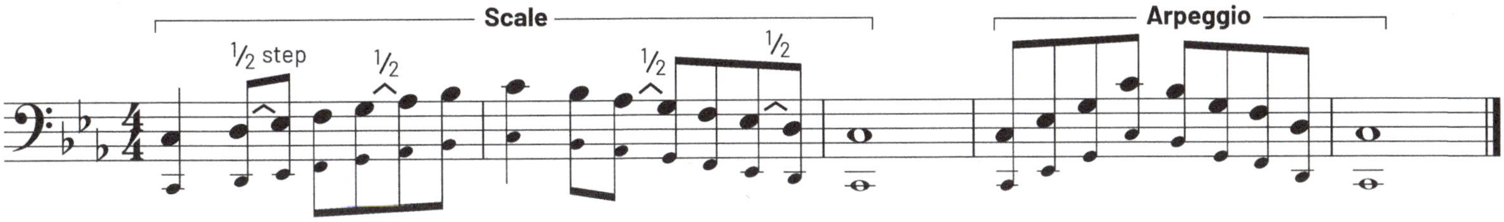

40. HARMONIC MINOR

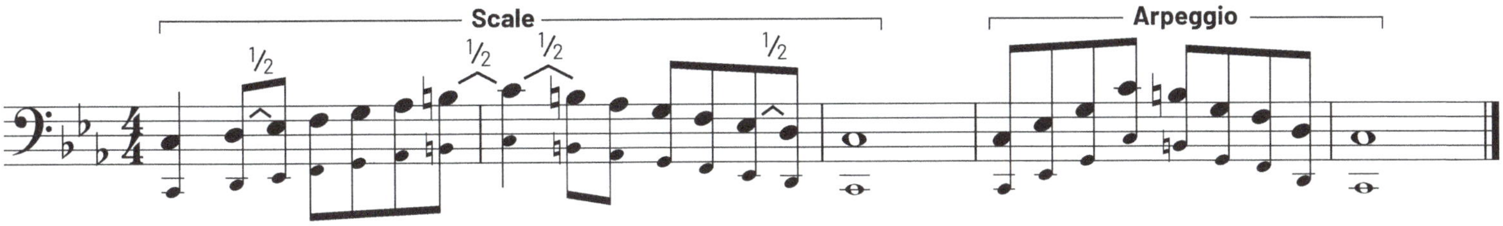

HISTORY

Even today, **Native American Indian music** continues to be an important part of tribal dancing ceremonies, using Apache fiddles, rattles, flutes, and log drums to accompany simple songs. American composer **Charles Wakefield Cadman** (1881–1946) wrote this song in 1914 based on Indian melodies he researched throughout his lifetime.

41. SONG OF THE WEEPING SPIRIT

Native American Indian Melody
Adapt. Charles Wakefield Cadman

Lento mysterioso ◄ *Slowly and mysteriously*

42. SCOTTISH LEGEND

Amy Marcy Beach

43. ESSENTIAL ELEMENTS QUIZ *Which measures sound major and which ones minor?*

Andante

F MAJOR

44. SCALE AND ARPEGGIO *Practice both upper and lower octaves.*

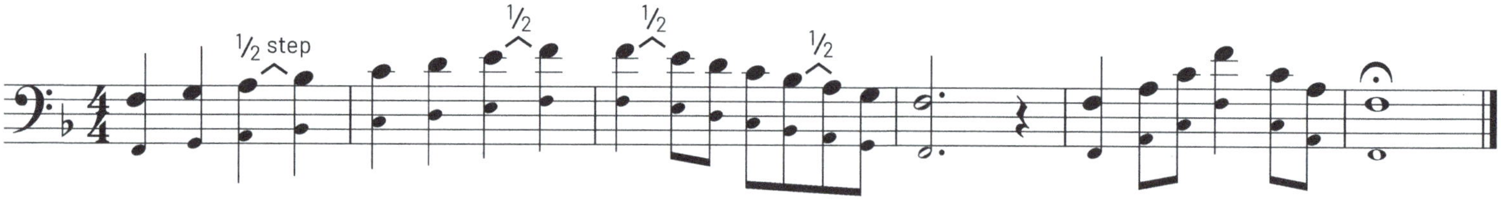

45. EXERCISE IN THIRDS

46. ARPEGGIO STUDY

47. TWO-PART ETUDE

48. CHROMATIC SCALE

49. BALANCE BUILDER

50. CHORALE

51. REST ALERT

52. RHYTHM RAP

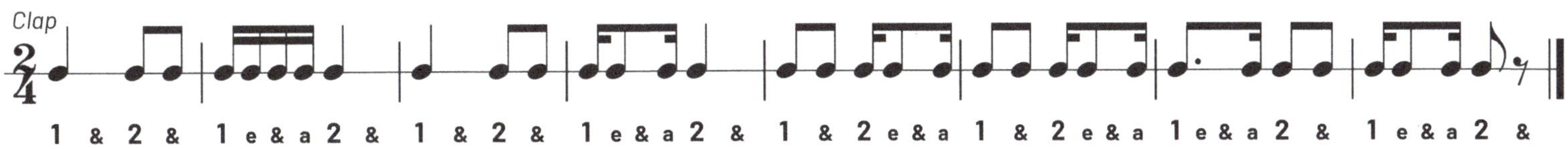

53. ISLAND SONG

French composer **Claude Debussy** (1862–1918) created moods and "impressions" with his music. While earlier composers used music to describe events (such as Tchaikovsky's *1812 Overture*), Debussy's new ideas helped shape today's music. The style of art and music created in this time is called "impressionism." The first automobile was produced during Debussy's lifetime. He died the same year that World War I ended.

HISTORY

54. THE LITTLE CHILD

Claude Debussy

Triplets with Rests

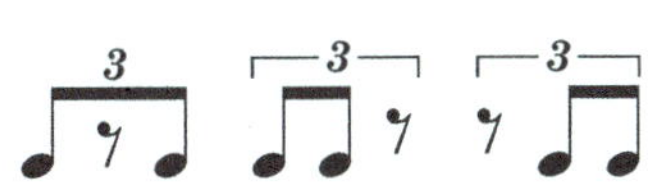

Triplets that start or end with a rest are usually marked with a bracket ⌐3⌐

THEORY

55. TRIPLET AND REST VARIATIONS

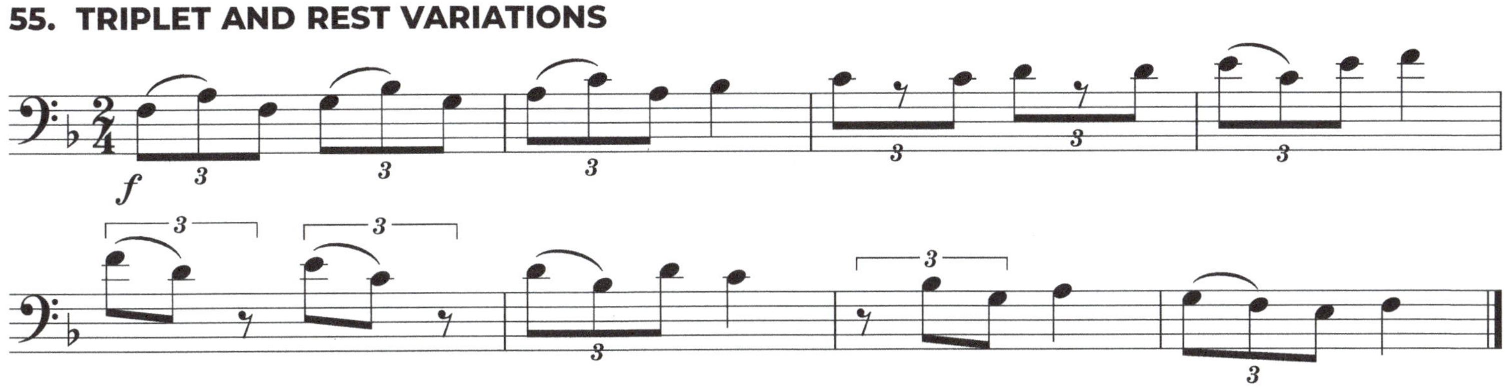

56. TURKEY IN THE STRAW

American Folk Song

57. ESSENTIAL ELEMENTS QUIZ *Write the first 2 lines of exercise 56 in cut time.*

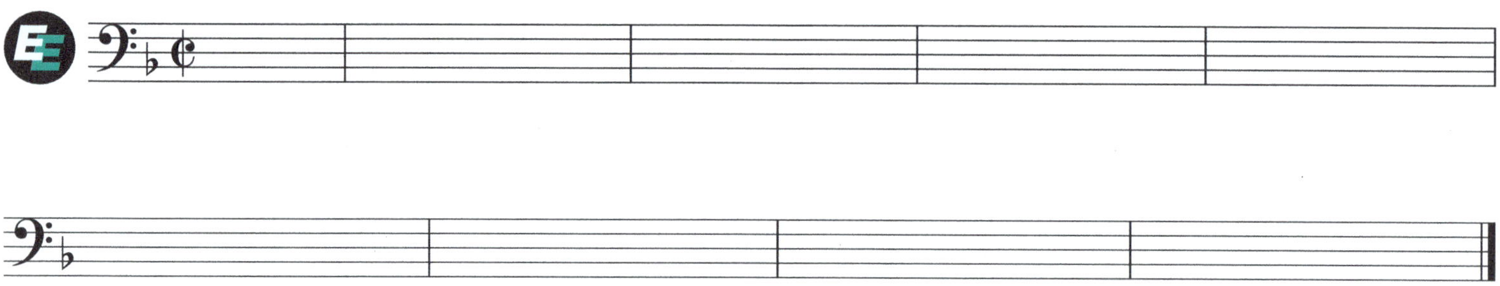

THEORY

Sixteenth Notes and Rests in $\frac{6}{8}$, $\frac{3}{8}$, $\frac{9}{8}$, $\frac{12}{8}$

𝅘𝅥𝅯 = 1/2 beat 𝄿 = 1/2 beat 𝅗𝅥 = 2 beats 𝄽 = 2 beats

𝅘𝅥𝅮 = 1 beat 𝄾 = 1 beat 𝅗𝅥. = 3 beats 𝄽. = 3 beats

58. RHYTHM RAP

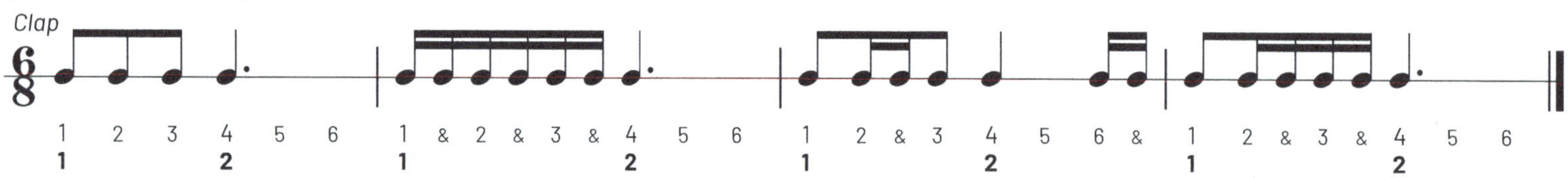

59. SONATINA

D MINOR

60. NATURAL MINOR *Practice both upper and lower octaves.*

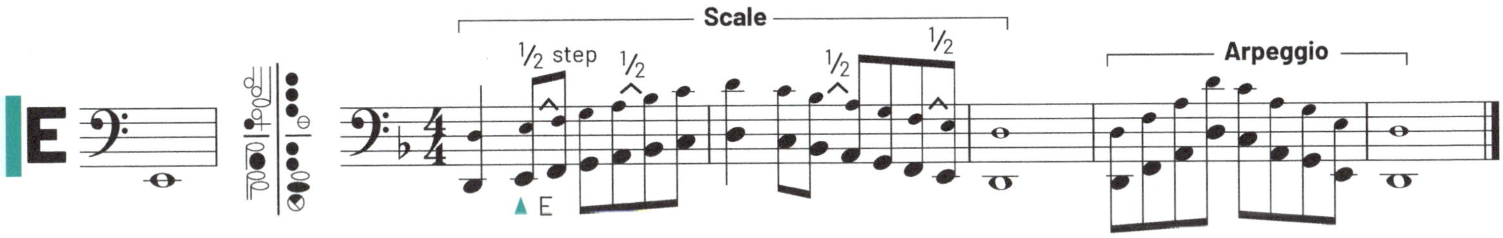

61. HARMONIC MINOR

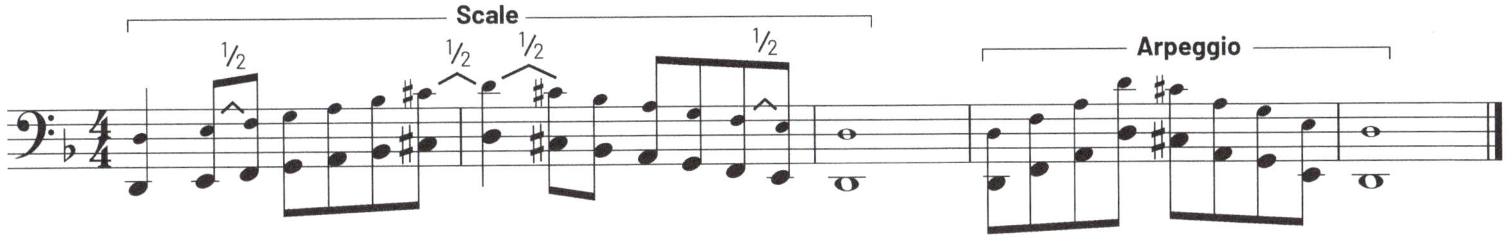

62. COSSACK MARCH

63. SLAVONIC DANCE NO. 2

Antonin Dvorák

64. ESSENTIAL ELEMENTS QUIZ – THE PRETTY GIRL

Irish

A♭ MAJOR

65. SCALE AND ARPEGGIO

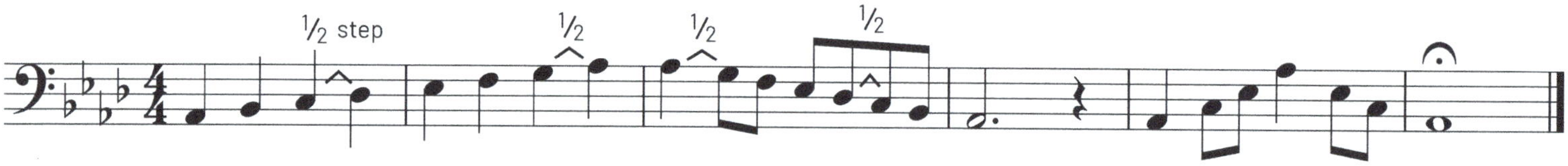

66. EXERCISE IN THIRDS

67. ARPEGGIO STUDY

68. TWO-PART ETUDE *Practice both upper and lower octaves.*

69. CHROMATIC SCALE

70. BALANCE BUILDER

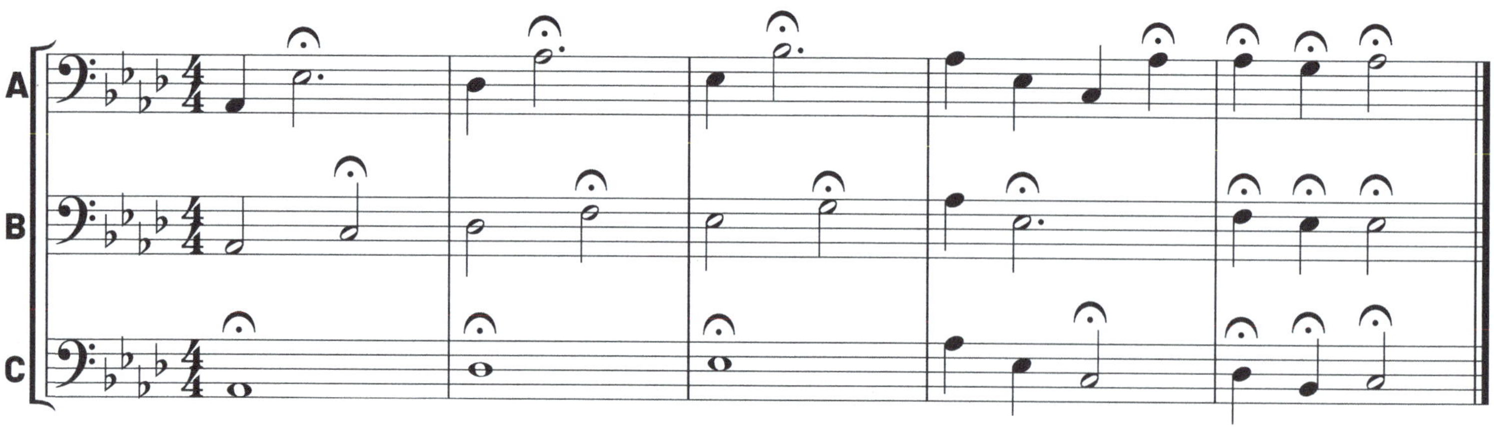

71. CHORALE

HISTORY

The Star Spangled Banner is the national anthem of the United States of America. Francis Scott Key wrote the words during the 1814 battle at Fort McHenry. He listened to the sounds of the fighting throughout the night while being detained on a ship. At dawn, he saw the American flag still flying over the fort. He was inspired to write these words, which were later set to the melody of a popular English song.

72. THE STAR SPANGLED BANNER

Words by Francis Scott Key
Music by John Stafford Smith

THEORY

Dynamics

pp – *pianissimo* (play very softly) ***ff*** – *fortissimo* (play very loudly)
Remember to use full breath support to produce the best possible tone and intonation.

73. INTERMEZZO

74. RHYTHM RAP

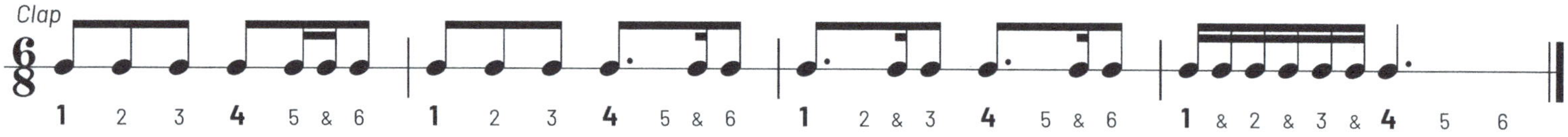

75. MORNING STAR

Moderato

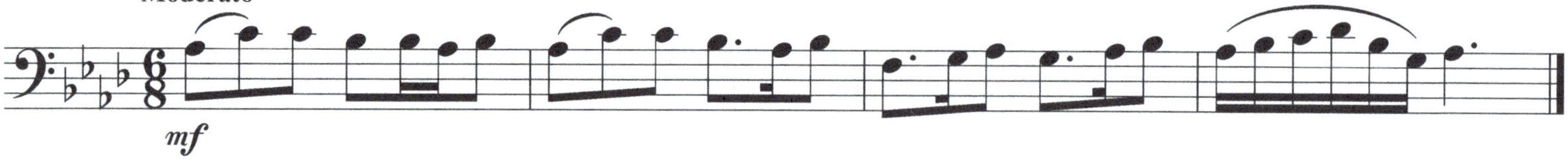

76. SONATA

Wolfgang Amadeus Mozart

Andante grazioso ◄ *Gracefully*

77. RONDEAU

Jean-Joseph Mouret

Allegro

THEORY

Grace Note A small note (or notes) which is played on, or slightly before the beat.

78. JULIET'S WALTZ

Charles Gounod

Tempo di valse

F MINOR

79. NATURAL MINOR *Practice both upper and lower octaves.*

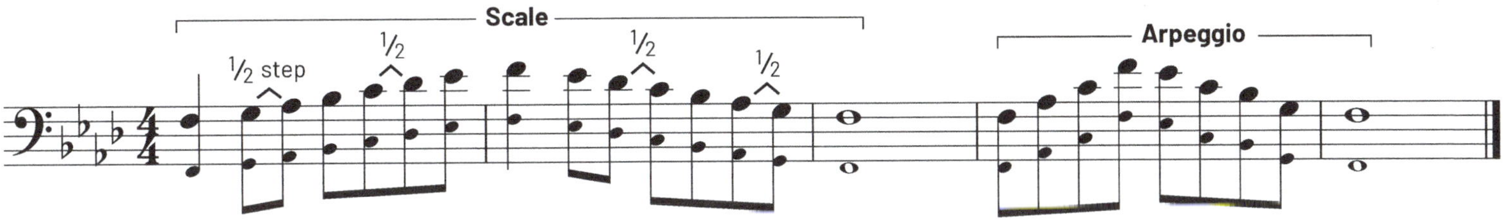

80. HARMONIC MINOR

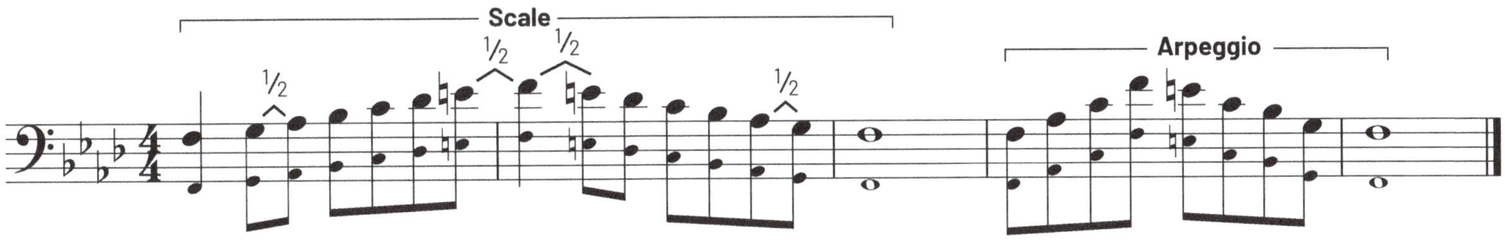

81. SORCERER'S APPRENTICE

Paul Dukas

82. I WALK THE ROAD AGAIN

American

83. ESSENTIAL ELEMENTS QUIZ – GREENSLEEVES

English Folk Song

C MAJOR

84. SCALE AND ARPEGGIO *Practice both upper and lower octaves.*

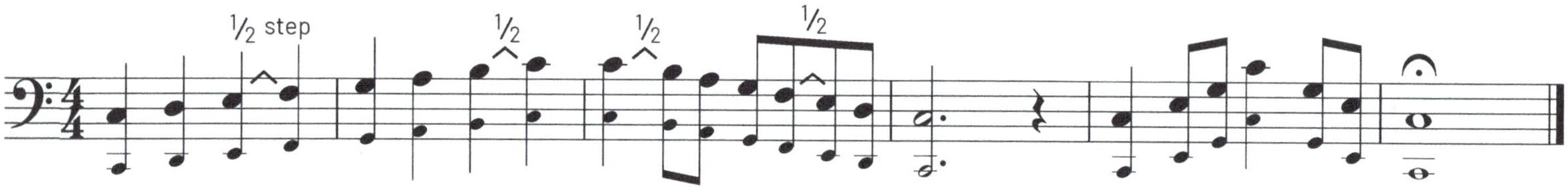

85. EXERCISE IN THIRDS

86. ARPEGGIO STUDY

87. TWO-PART ETUDE

88. CHROMATIC SCALE

89. BALANCE BUILDER

90. CHORALE

African American spirituals originated in the 1700's. As one of the largest categories of true American folk music, these melodies were sung and passed on for generations without being written down. Black and white people worked together to publish the first spiritual collection in 1867, four years after *The Emancipation Proclamation* was signed into law.

91. SIT DOWN, SISTER

African American Spiritual

92. SPINNING SONG – Duet

Johann Ellmenreich

THEORY

Quarter Note Triplets

Similar to eighth note triplets where 1 beat is divided into 3 equal notes,

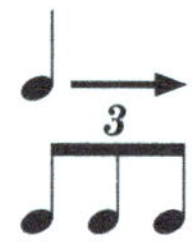

quarter note triplets divide 2 beats into 3 equal notes.

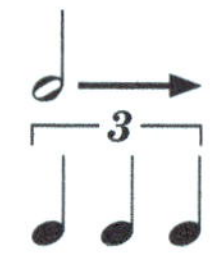

93. RHYTHM RAP

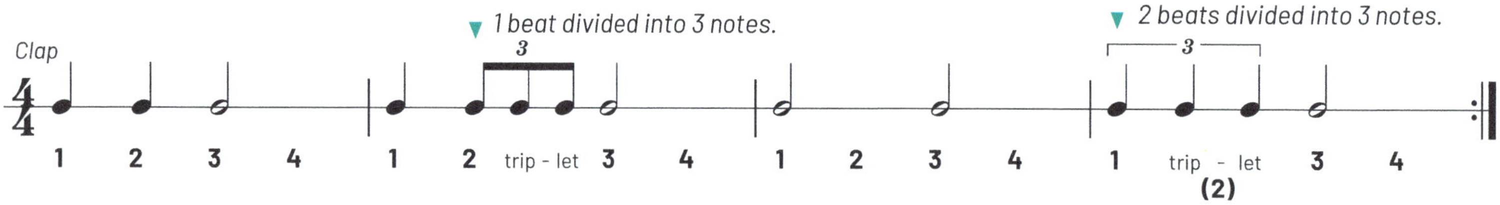

94. THREE FOR TWO

95. SURIRAM'S SONG

Malaysian Folk Song

HISTORY

Africa is a large continent that is made up of many nations, and **African folk music** is as diverse as its many cultures. Folk songs from any country are expressions of work, love, war, sadness, and joy. This song is from Tanzania. The words describe a rabbit hopping and running through a field. Listen to the percussion section play African-sounding drums and rhythms.

96. JIBULI (The Rabbit's Song)

Adapted Tanzanian Folk Song

A MINOR

97. NATURAL MINOR

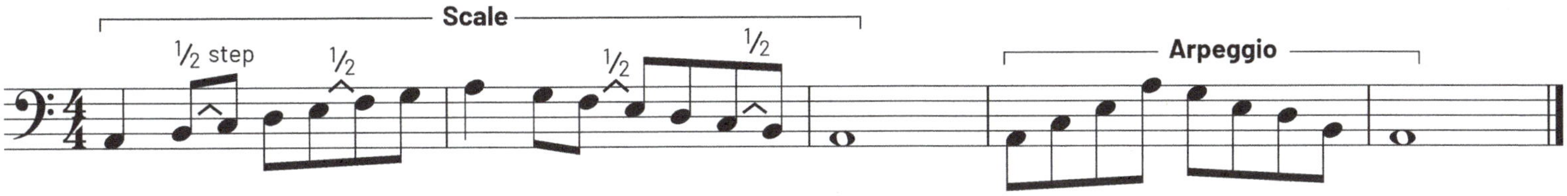

98. HARMONIC MINOR

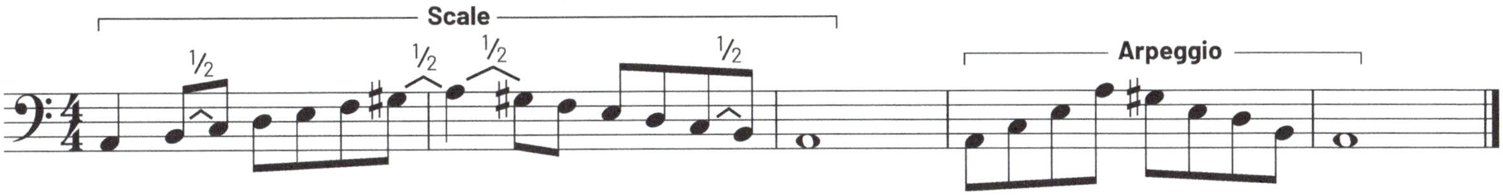

THEORY

Meter Changes

Meter changes, or changing time signatures within a section of music, are commonly found in contemporary music. Composers use this technique to create a unique rhythm, pulse, or musical style.

99. TIME ZONES

HISTORY

Important French composers of the late 19th century include **Claude Debussy** (1862–1918), **Gabriel Fauré** (1845–1924), **Erik Satie** (1866–1925), **César Franck** (1822–1890), **Camille Saint-Saëns** (1835–1921), and **Paul Dukas** (1865–1935). Their works continue to have influence on the music of modern day composers. Gabriel Fauré wrote *Pavanne* (originally for orchestra) in 1887, two years before the Eiffel Tower was completed in Paris.

100. PAVANNE

Gabriel Fauré

D♭ MAJOR

101. SCALE AND ARPEGGIO *Practice both upper and lower octaves.*

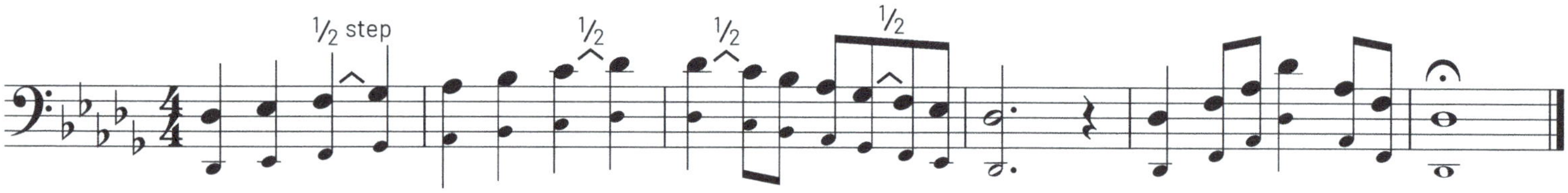

102. EXERCISE IN THIRDS

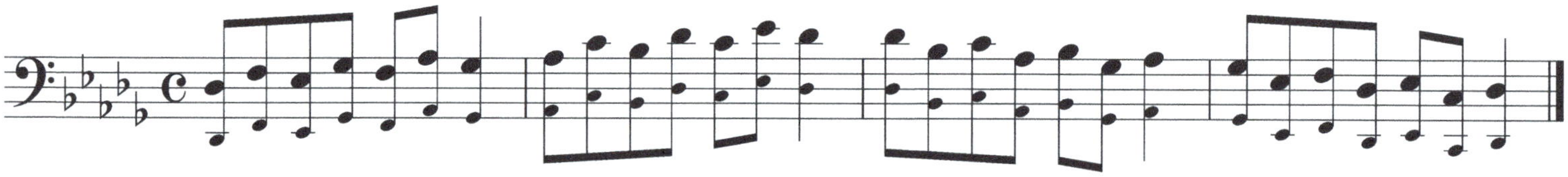

103. ARPEGGIO STUDY

104. TWO-PART ETUDE

105. CHROMATIC SCALE

106. BALANCE BUILDER

107. CHORALE

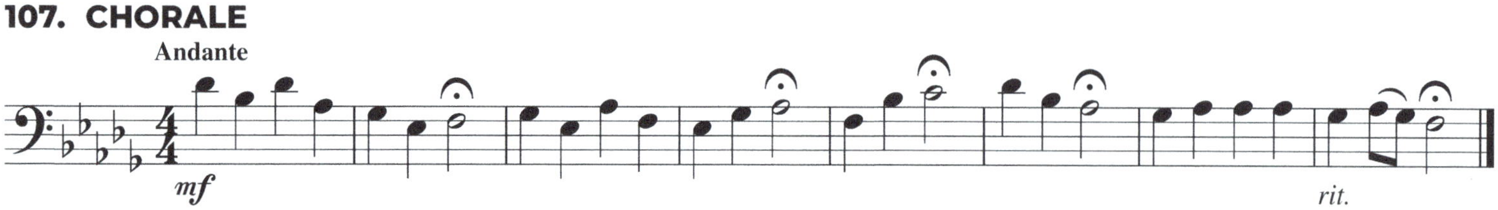

*When moving to or from middle A♭, use the alternate D♭ fingering.

108. GERMAN NATIONAL ANTHEM

Franz Josef Haydn

109. JOY

Johann Sebastian Bach

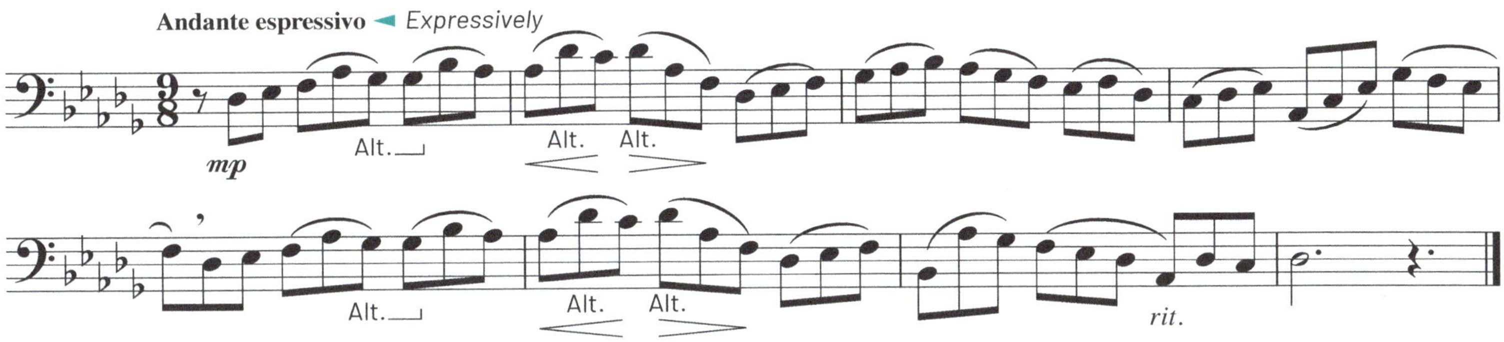

$\frac{5}{4}$ Time Signature

= **5 beats** per measure
= **Quarter** note gets one beat

Conducting

Practice conducting these five-beat patterns.

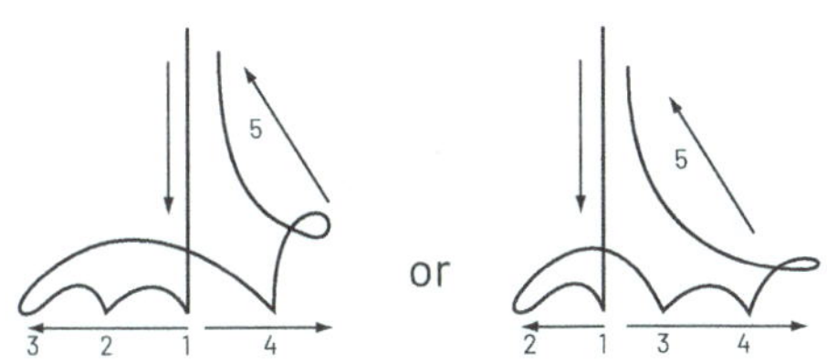

THEORY

110. RHYTHM RAP

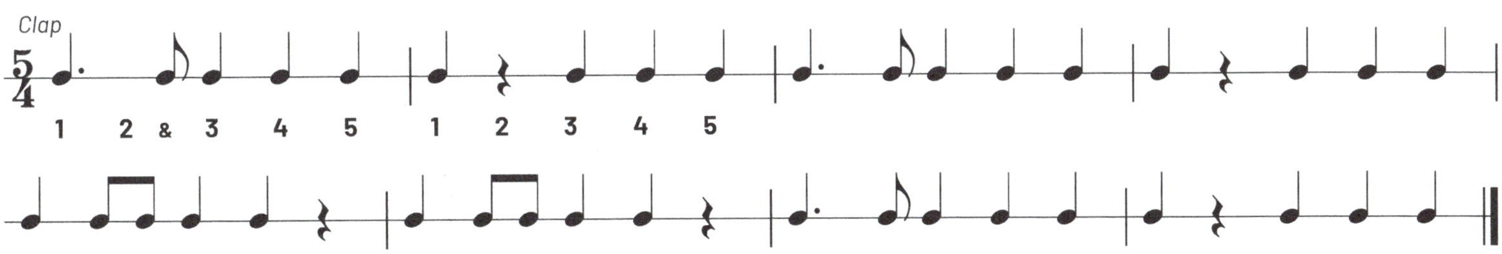

111. LET'S COUNT FIVE

*Alternate G♭ (F♯) should be used when moving to or from B♭ or D♭.

112. SUKURU ITO

African Folk Song

Moderato

HISTORY

English composer **George Frideric Handel** (1685-1759) lived during the **Baroque Period (1600-1750)**. *Water Music* was written in honor of England's King George I. The first performance took place on the Thames River on July 17, 1717. Fifty musicians performed the work while floating on a barge. Handel lived during the same time as Johann Sebastian Bach, perhaps the most famous Baroque composer.

113. WATER MUSIC

George Frideric Handel

Allegro maestoso

114. ESSENTIAL TECHNIQUE QUIZ – PICTURES AT AN EXHIBITION

Modeste Mussorgsky

Maestoso

B♭ MINOR

115. NATURAL MINOR *Practice both upper and lower octaves.*

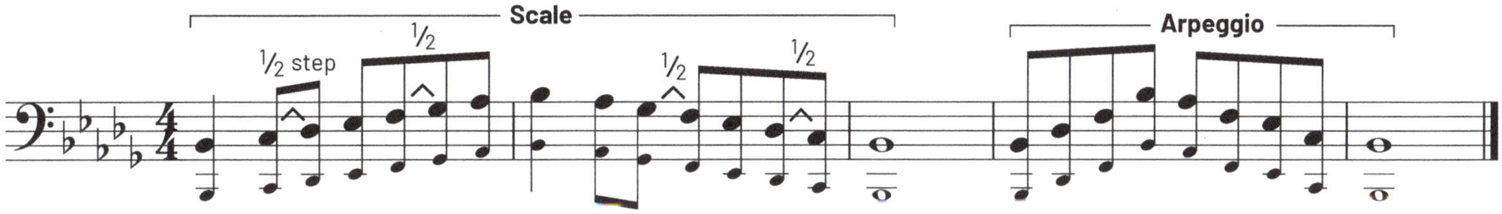

116. HARMONIC MINOR

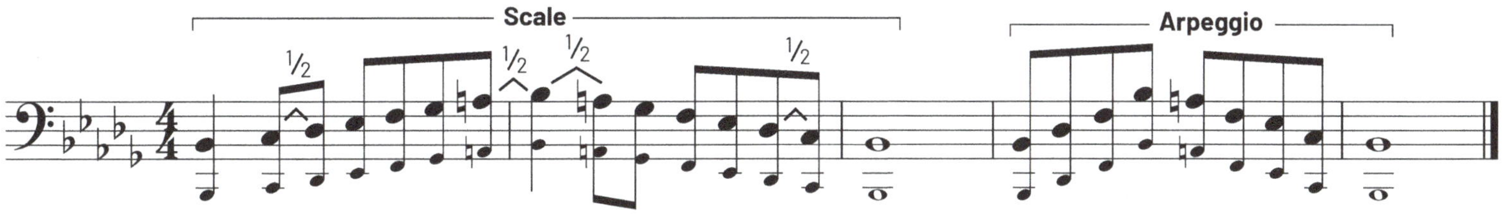

Ostinato A clear and distinct musical phrase that is repeated persistently.

British composer **Gustav Holst** (1874–1934) is one of the most widely played composers for concert band today. Many of his compositions, including his familiar military suites, are based on tuneful English folk songs. His most famous work for orchestra, *The Planets* (1916), has seven movements—one written for each known planet, excluding Earth.

117. MARS – Duet/Trio

Gustav Holst

G MAJOR

118. SCALE AND ARPEGGIO *Practice both upper and lower octaves.*

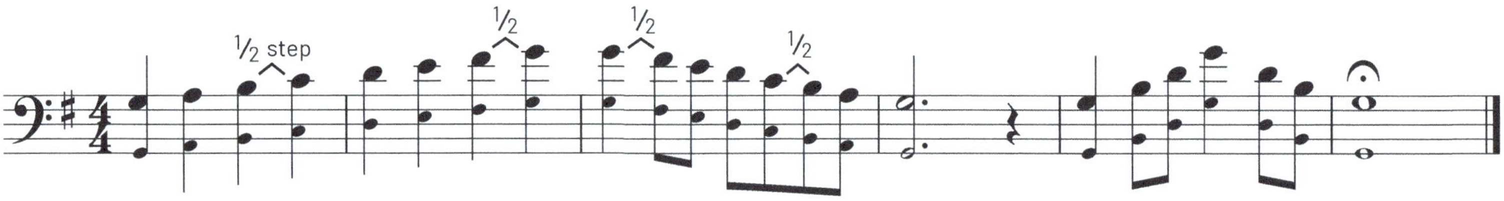

119. EXERCISE IN THIRDS

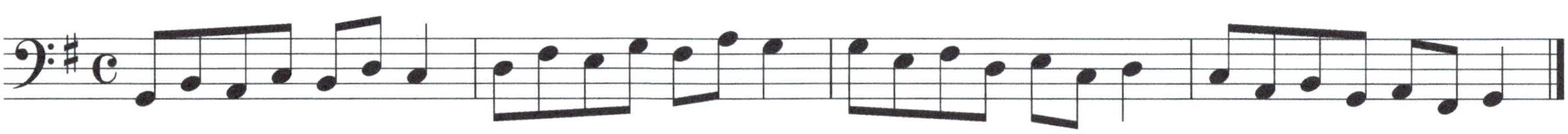

120. ARPEGGIO STUDY

121. TWO-PART ETUDE

122. CHROMATIC SCALE

123. BALANCE BUILDER

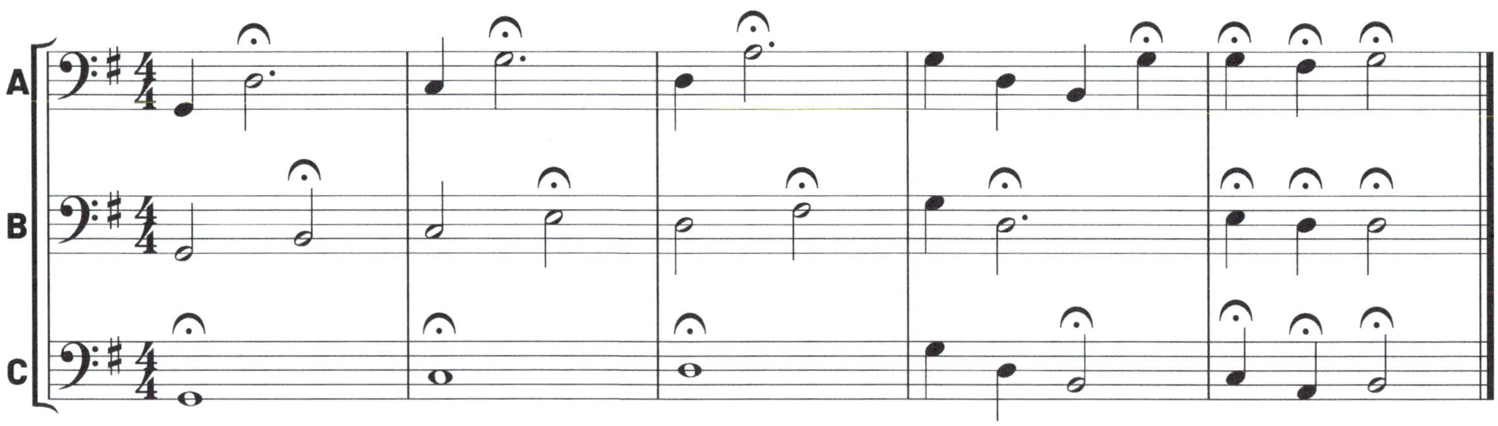

124. CHORALE

Norwegian composer **Edvard Grieg** (1843–1907) based much of his music on the folk songs and dances of Norway. During the late 19th century, composers often used melodies from their native land. This trend is called **nationalism**. Russian **Modeste Mussorgsky** (1839–1881), Czech **Antonin Dvořák** (1841–1904), and Englishman **Sir Edward Elgar** (1857–1934) are other famous composers whose music was influenced by nationalism.

HISTORY

125. NORWEGIAN DANCE

Edvard Grieg

Andante

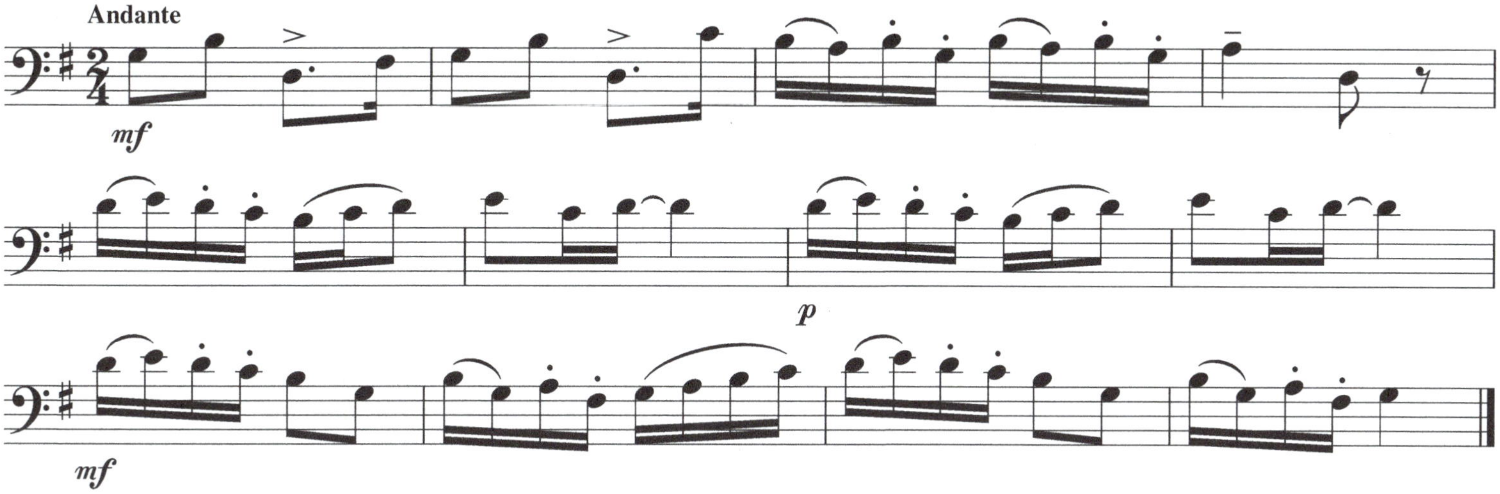

126. FRENCH NATIONAL ANTHEM (LA MARSEILLAISE)

Rouget De L'Isle

Allegro marziale ◄ *March-like style*

Music written during the **Renaissance Period (1430–1600)** was often upbeat and dance-like. *Wolsey's Wilde* was originally written for the lute, an ancestor to the guitar and the most popular instrument of the Renaissance era. Modern day concert band composer Gordon Jacob used this popular song in his *William Byrd Suite*, written as a tribute to English composer William Byrd (1543–1623).

HISTORY

127. WOLSEY'S WILDE

Anonymous

Animato ◄ *Animated, lively*

E MINOR

128. NATURAL MINOR *Practice both upper and lower octaves.*

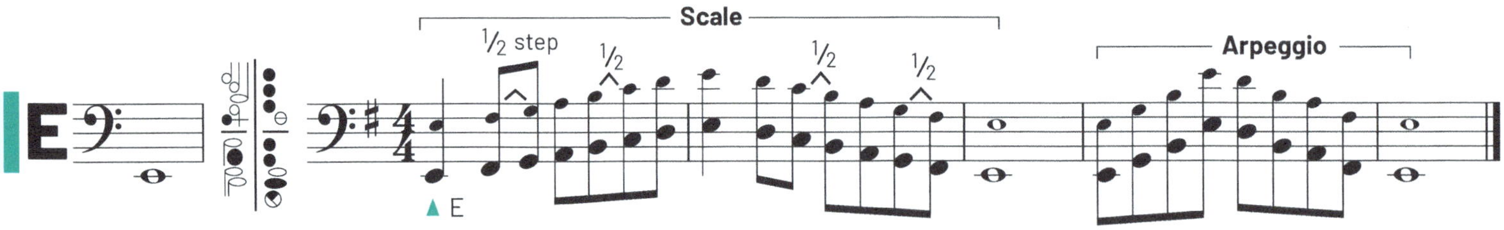

129. HARMONIC MINOR

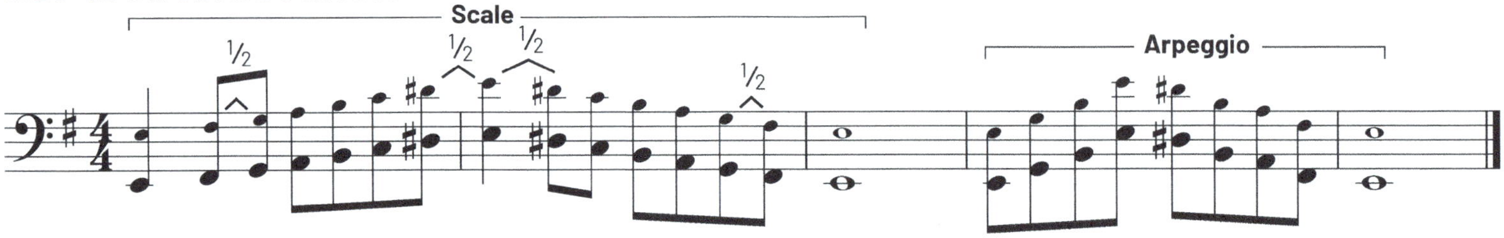

HISTORY

Native Japanese instruments include the *shakuhachi*, a bamboo flute played pointing downward; the *koto*, a long zither with movable frets played sitting down; and the *gakubiwa*, a pear-shaped lute with strings that are plucked. These instruments have been an important part of Japanese culture since the 8th century. *Kabuki*, a Japanese theatrical form that originated in 1603, remains popular in Japan. Performers play native Japanese instruments during Kabuki performances.

130. SONG OF THE SHAKUHACHI

Japanese Folk Song

THEORY

D.C. al Coda — At the **D.C. al Coda**, play again from the beginning to the indication **To Coda** ⊕, then skip to the section marked ⊕ **Coda**, meaning "ending section."

D.S. al Coda — Similar to **D.C. al Coda**, but return to the sign 𝄋.

131. POLOVETZIAN DANCES

Alexander Borodin

Looking for some more fun music to play?
See the inside front cover for instructions on accessing recent popular Bonus Songs.

D MAJOR

132. SCALE AND ARPEGGIO *Practice both upper and lower octaves.*

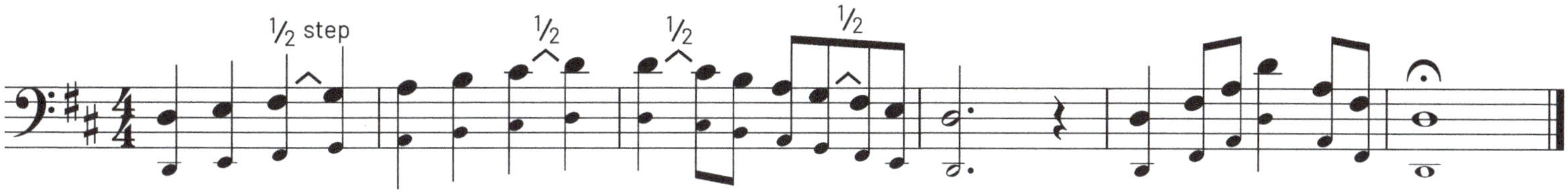

133. EXERCISE IN THIRDS

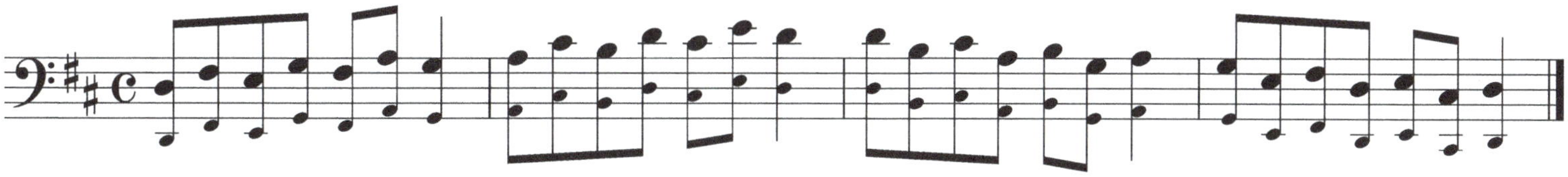

134. ARPEGGIO STUDY

135. TWO-PART ETUDE

136. CHORALE

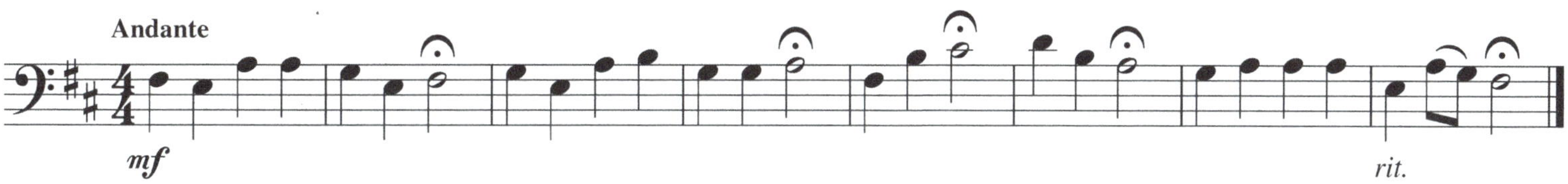

B MINOR

137. NATURAL MINOR

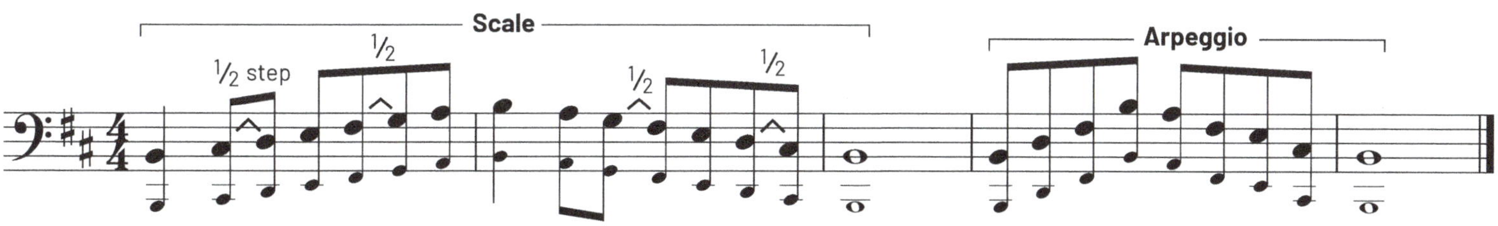

138. HARMONIC MINOR

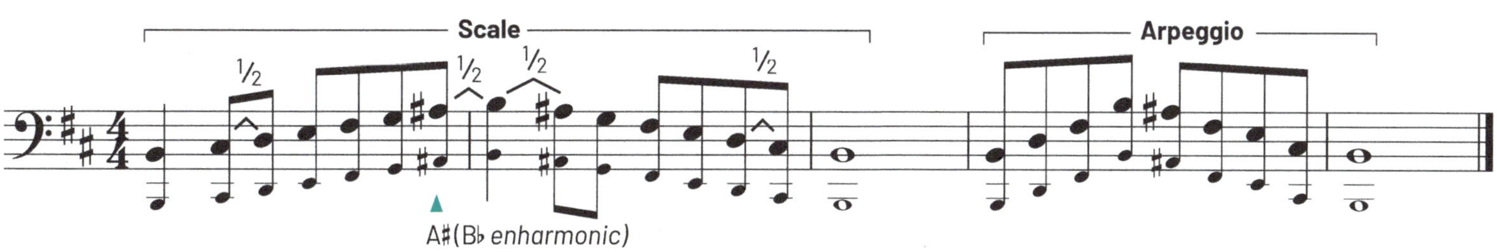

HISTORY

Latin American music combines the folk music from South and Central America, the Caribbean Islands, American Indian, Spanish, and Portuguese cultures. Melodies are often accompanied by drums, maracas, and claves. Latin American music continues to influence jazz, classical, and popular styles of music. *Cielito Lindo* is a Latin American love song.

139. CIELITO LINDO

C. Fernandez

HISTORY

Tchaikovsky, along with Wagner, Brahms, Mendelssohn, and Chopin, helped define the musical era known as the **Romantic Period (1825–1900)**. The "symphonic tone poem" from this period continues to be one of the most popular musical forms performed by orchestras and bands today.

140. WALTZ IN FIVE (from SYMPHONY NO. 6)

Peter I. Tchaikovsky

141. THE YOUNG CHEVALIER

Scottish

G♭ MAJOR

142. SCALE AND ARPEGGIO *Practice both upper and lower octaves.*

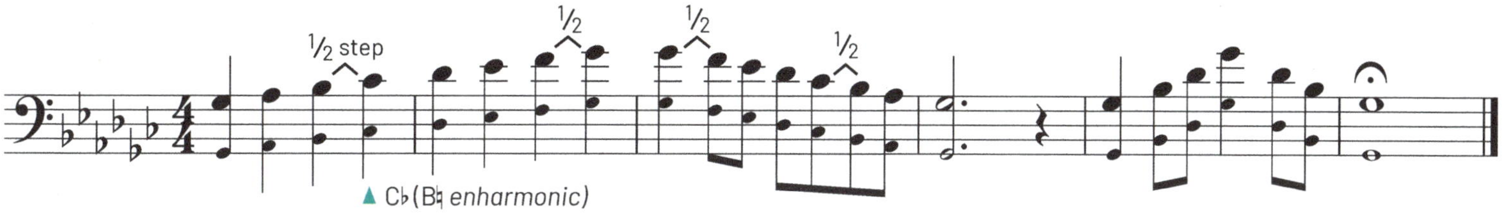

143. EXERCISE IN THIRDS

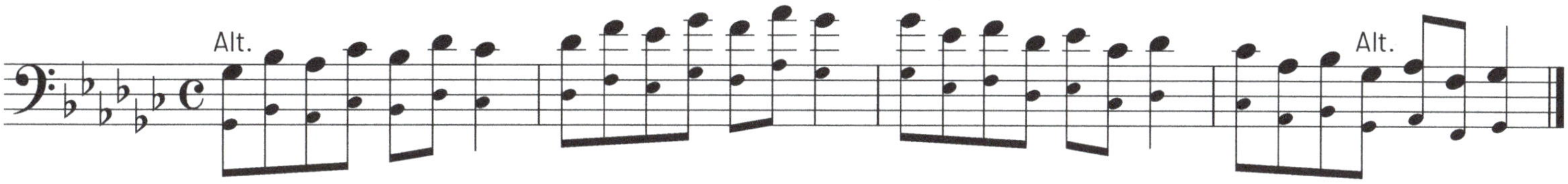

144. ARPEGGIO STUDY

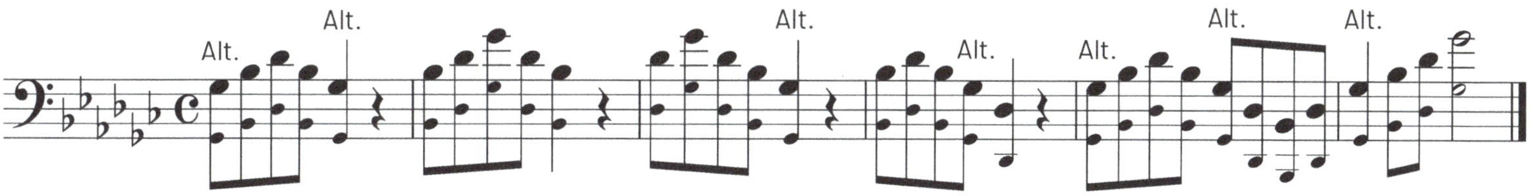

145. TWO-PART ETUDE

146. CHORALE

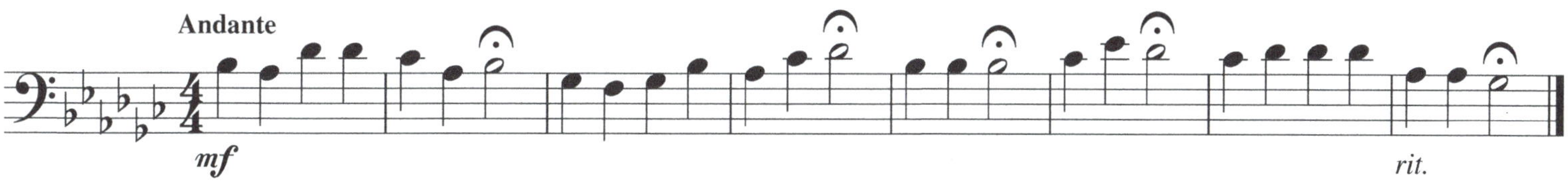

E♭ MINOR

147. NATURAL MINOR

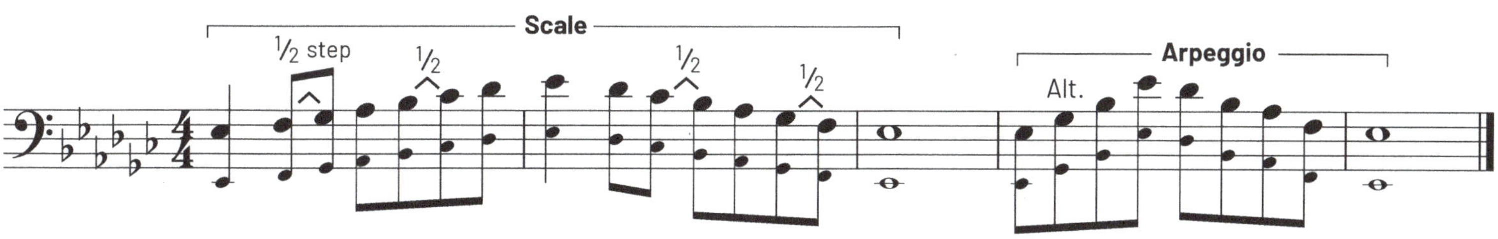

148. HARMONIC MINOR

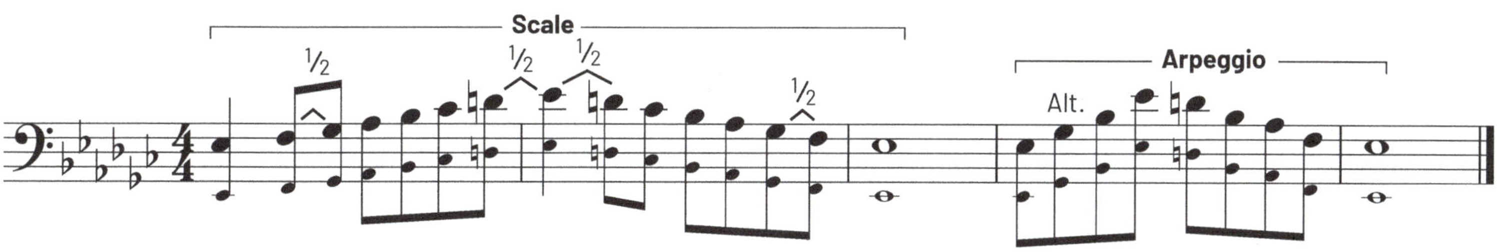

INDIVIDUAL STUDY – Bassoon

149. STUDY IN C MAJOR

150. EXPRESSION STUDY

151. STACCATO ETUDE

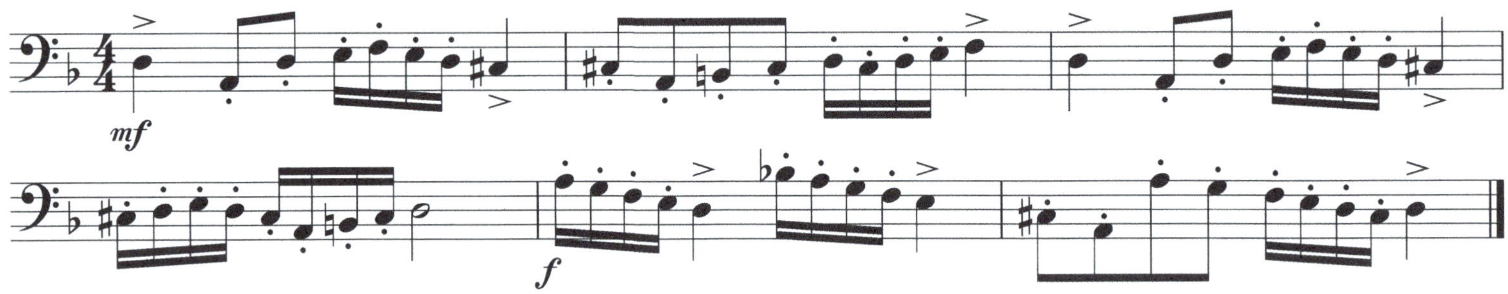

152. LEGATO STUDY IN F MINOR

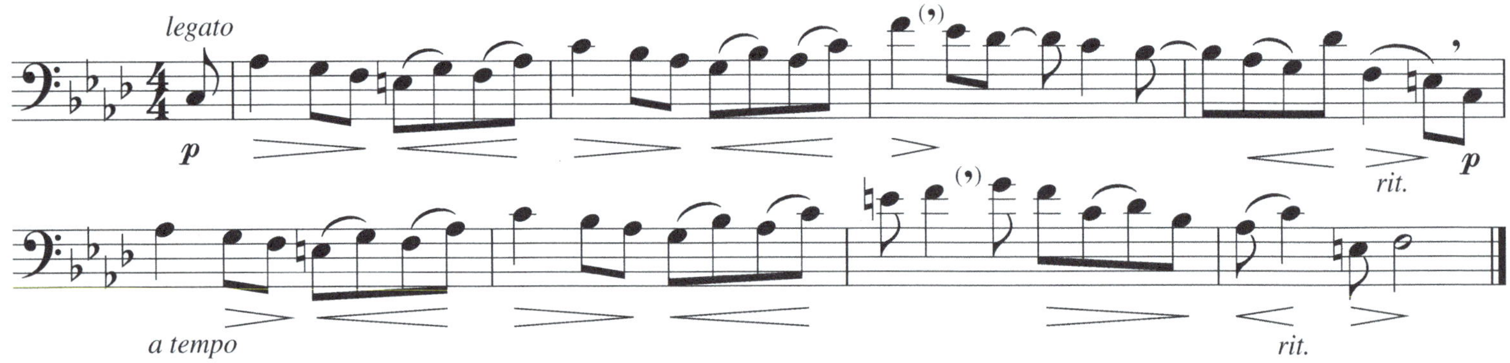

153. EXERCISE IN D MINOR

INDIVIDUAL STUDY – Bassoon

154. TRIPLET WORKOUT

155. C MINOR EXERCISE

156. STUDY IN 12/8

157. STUDY IN G MAJOR

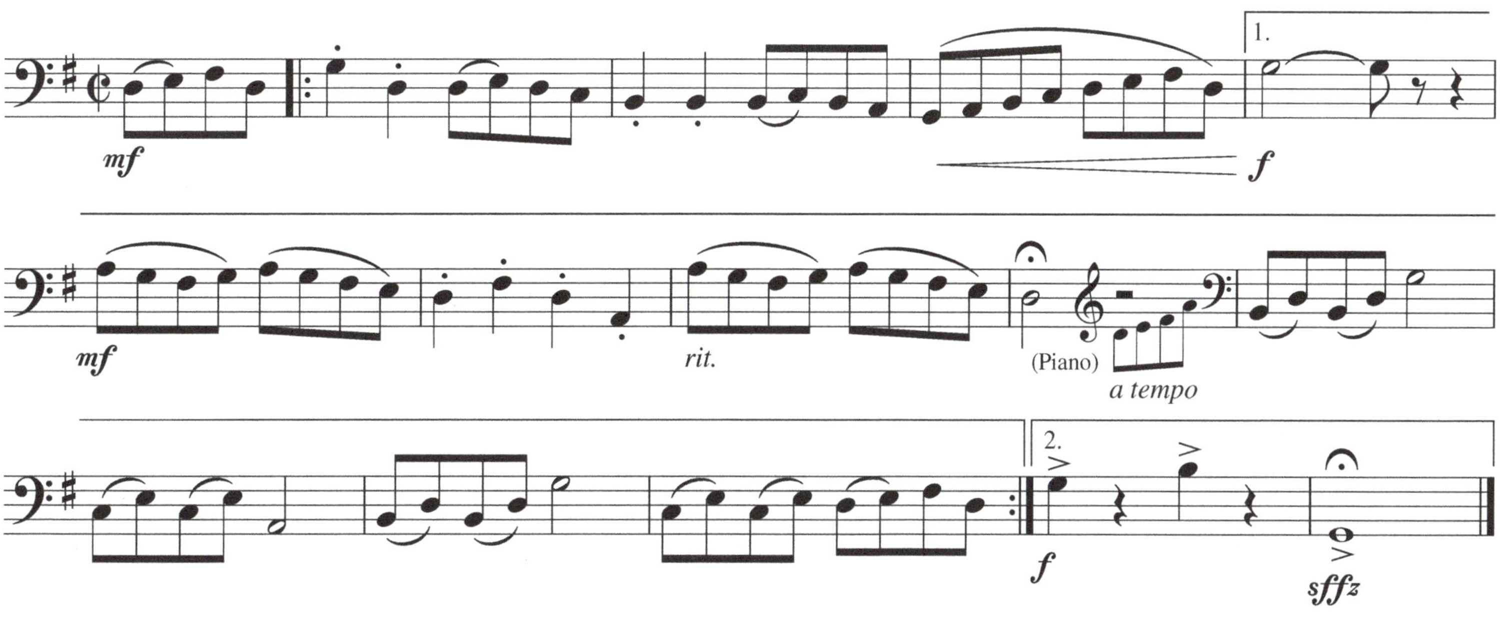

READING SKILL BUILDERS

158. READING SKILL BUILDER NO. 1

159. READING SKILL BUILDER NO. 2

160. READING SKILL BUILDER NO. 3

161. READING SKILL BUILDER NO. 4

162. READING SKILL BUILDER NO. 5

READING SKILL BUILDERS

163. READING SKILL BUILDER NO. 6

164. READING SKILL BUILDER NO. 7

165. READING SKILL BUILDER NO. 8

166. READING SKILL BUILDER NO. 9

167. CHORALE (Prelude from Hansel and Gretel)

Engelbert Humperdinck
Arr. by John Higgins

168. CHORALE (Based on a Theme by Palestrina)

Arr. by John Higgins

169. CHORALE (Based on a Theme by J. S. Bach)

Arr. by John Higgins

170. CHORALE (Based on a Theme by Tchaikovsky)

Arr. by John Higgins

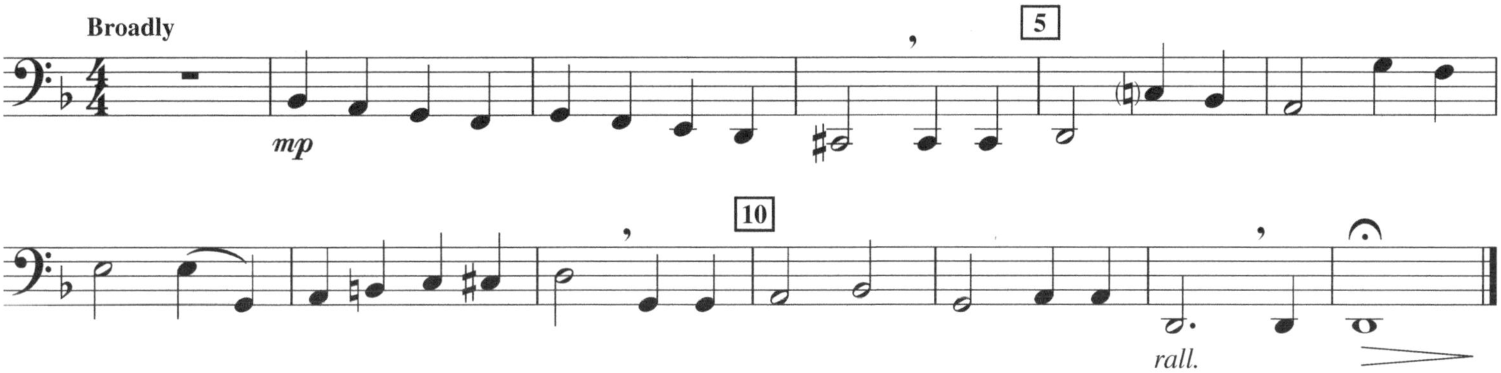

171. CHORALE (Erhalt Uns In Der Wahrheit)

Johann Sebastian Bach
Arr. by John Higgins

172. CHORALE (Navy Hymn)

John Dykes
Arr. by John Higgins

173. CHORALE (Prelude)

Frederic Chopin
Arr. by John Higgins

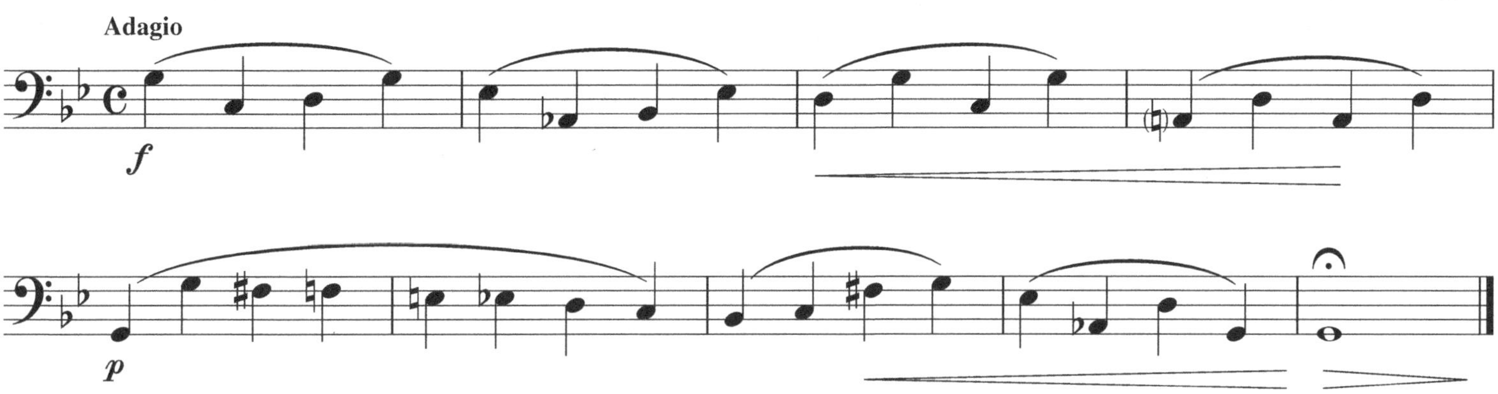

RHYTHM STUDIES

RHYTHM STUDIES

THE BASICS OF JAZZ STYLE from Essential Elements for Jazz Ensemble

Accenting "2 and 4"

For most traditional music the important beats in 4/4 time are 1 and 3. In jazz, however, the emphasis is usually on beats 2 and 4. Emphasizing "2 and 4" gives the music a jazz feeling.

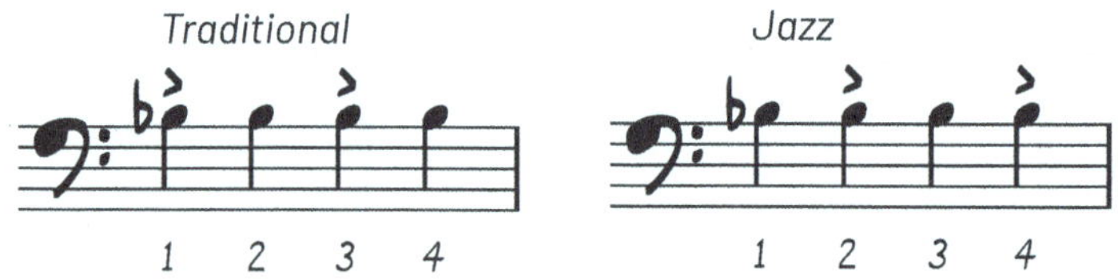

174. ACCENTING 2 AND 4

Jazz Articulations

There are four basic articulations in jazz.

Tenuto (full value) | **Staccato** (short, unaccented) | **Long Accent** (full value, accented) | **Roof Top Accent** (short, accented)

Swing 8th Notes Sound Different Than They Look

In swing, the 2nd 8th note of each beat is actually played like the last third of a triplet, and slightly accented. 8th notes in swing style are usually played *legato*.

175. SWING 8TH NOTES

Quarter Notes

Quarter notes in swing style are usually played detached (*staccato*) with accents on beats 2 and 4.

176. QUARTERS AND 8THS

177. RUNNIN' AROUND

Syncopation in Jazz

When beats are played early (anticipated) or played late (delayed), the music becomes syncopated. Syncopation makes the music sound "jazzy."

178. WHEN THE SAINTS GO MARCHING IN – Without Syncopation

James Black and Katherine Purvis

179. WHEN THE SAINTS GO MARCHING IN – With Syncopation

"Jazzin' Up" the Melody by Adding Rhythms

Adding rhythms to a melody is another easy way to improvise in a jazz style. Start by filling out long notes with repeated 8th and quarter notes. Remember to swing the 8th notes (play *legato* and give the upbeats an accent).

180. "JAZZIN' UP" JINGLE BELLS

J. Pierpont

MAKE UP YOUR OWN (IMPROVISE)

181. LONDON BRIDGE

Complete the melody in your own "jazzed up" way. Use only the notes shown in parentheses. Slashes on the staff indicate when to improvise.

Major Scales

Play major scales as part of your daily practice routine. Play all octaves, keys, and arpeggios at various dynamic levels and tempos. Keep a steady pulse. Try different articulation patterns, such as:

A. **B.** **C.**

182. B♭ MAJOR

183. E♭ MAJOR

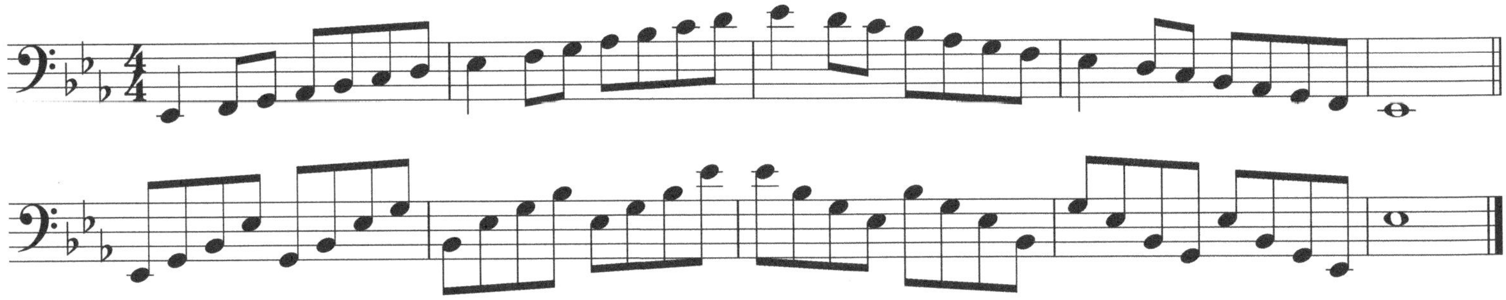

184. F MAJOR

185. C MAJOR

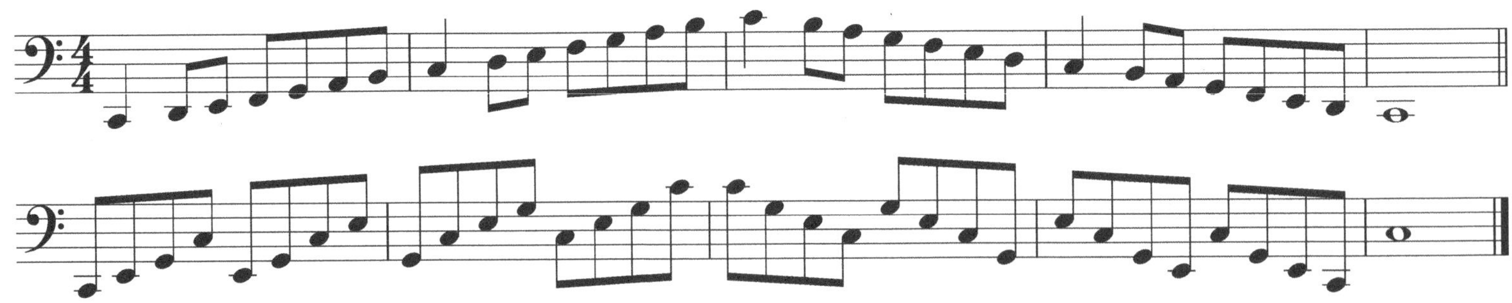

186. A♭ MAJOR

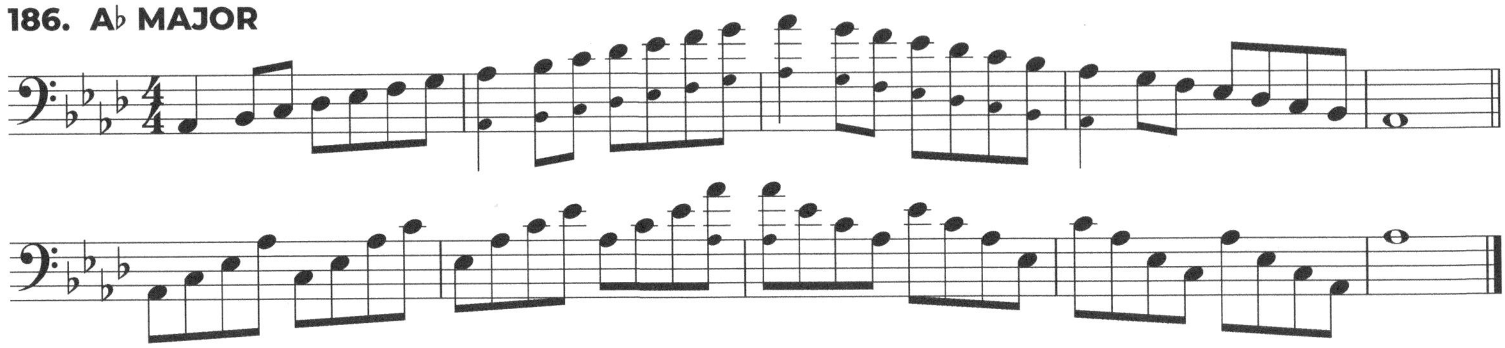

187. D♭ MAJOR

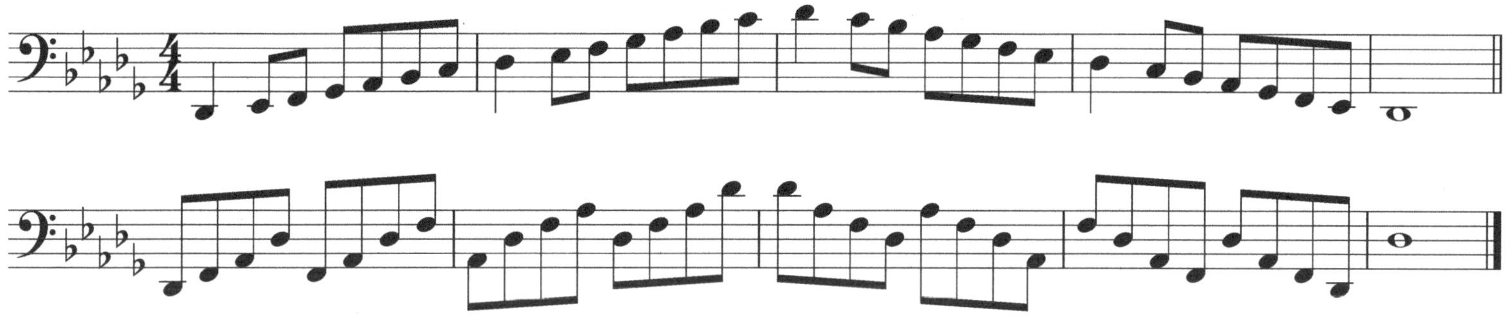

188. G MAJOR

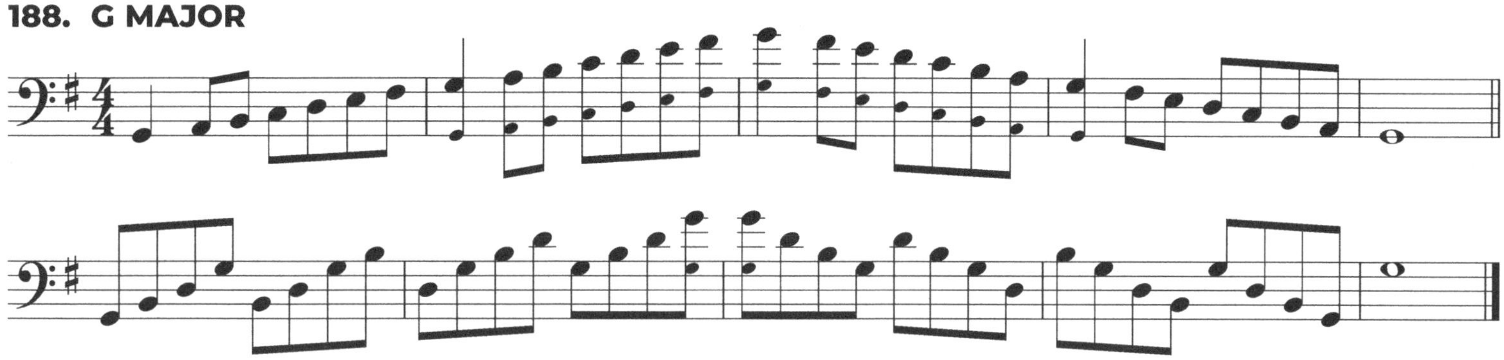

189. D MAJOR

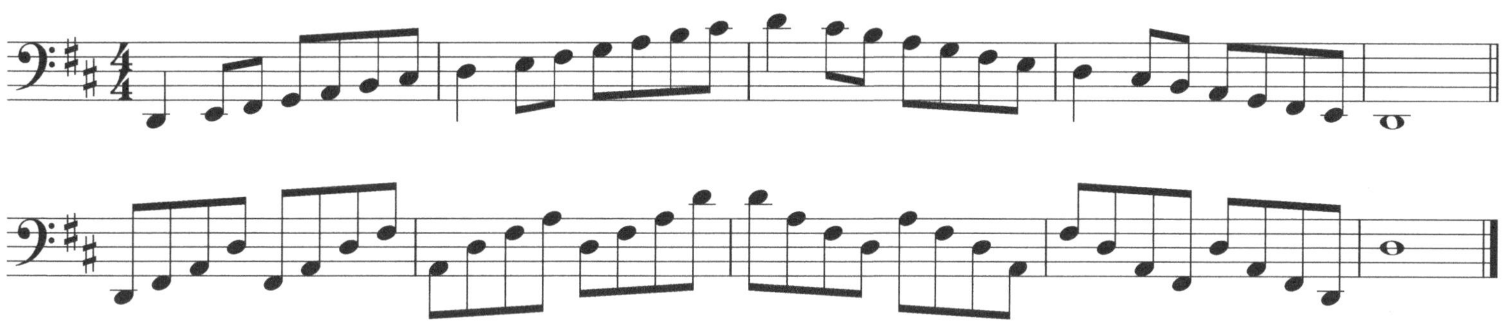

190. A MAJOR

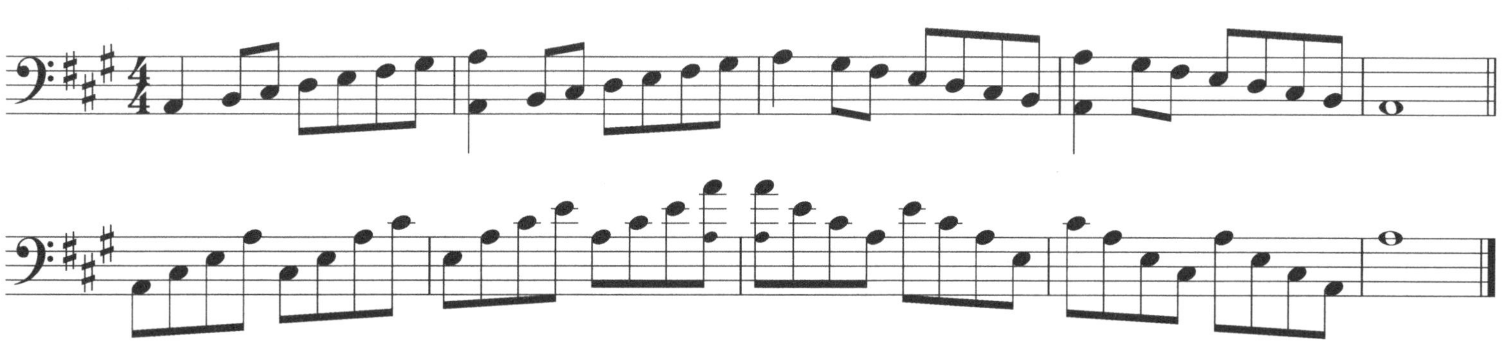

191. G♭ MAJOR

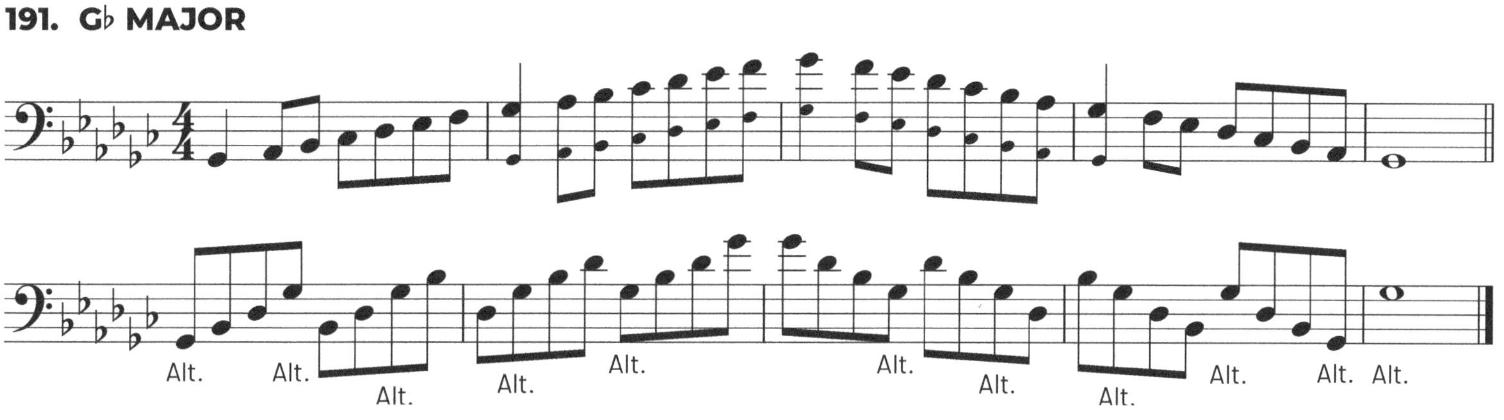

Minor Scales

Play minor scales as part of your daily practice routine. Play all octaves, all three forms, and the arpeggios at various dynamic levels and tempos. Keep a steady pulse. Try different articulation patterns, such as:

192. D MINOR SCALE

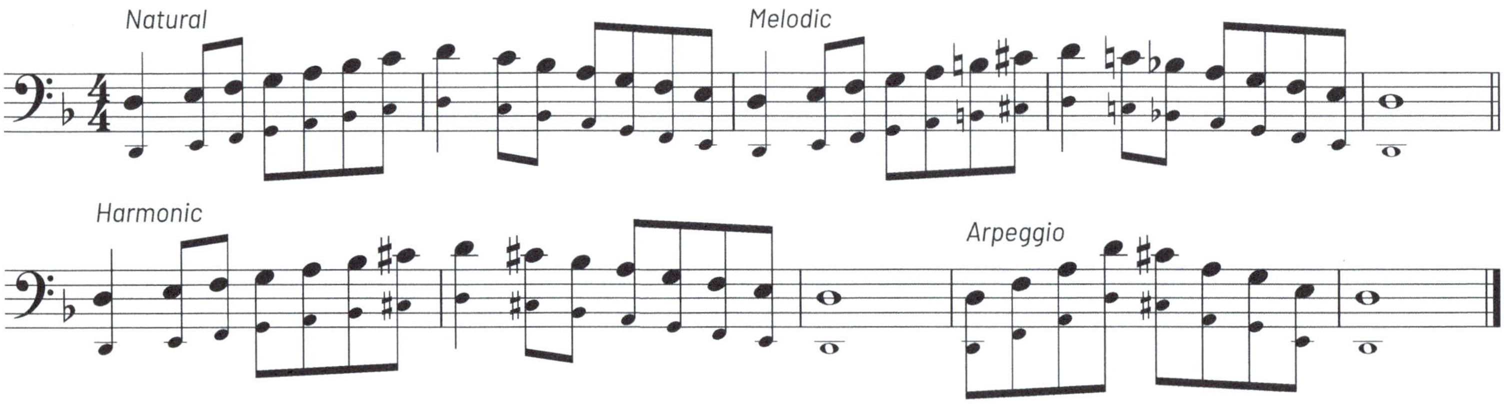

193. G MINOR SCALE

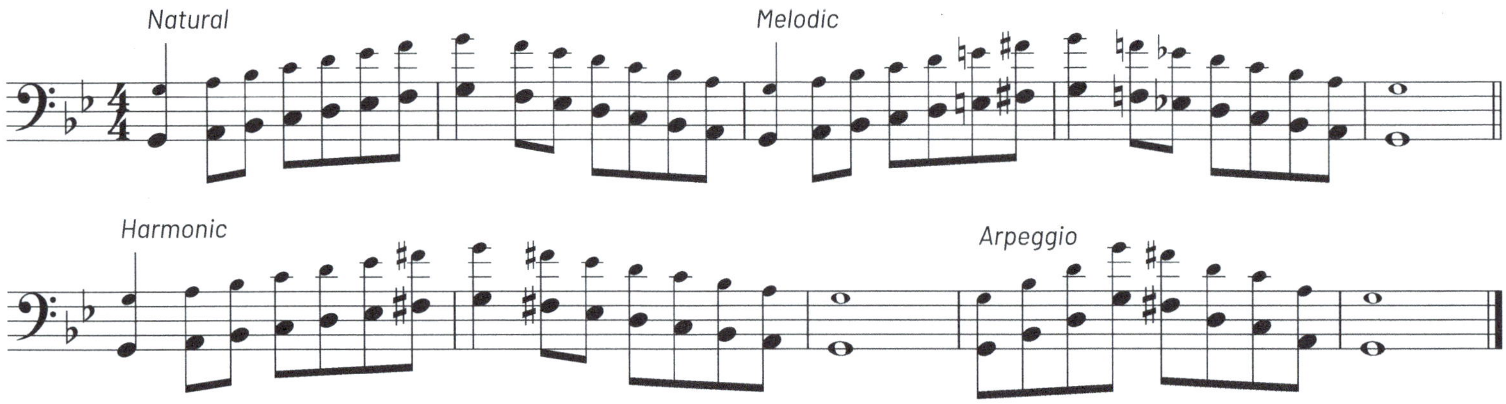

194. C MINOR SCALE

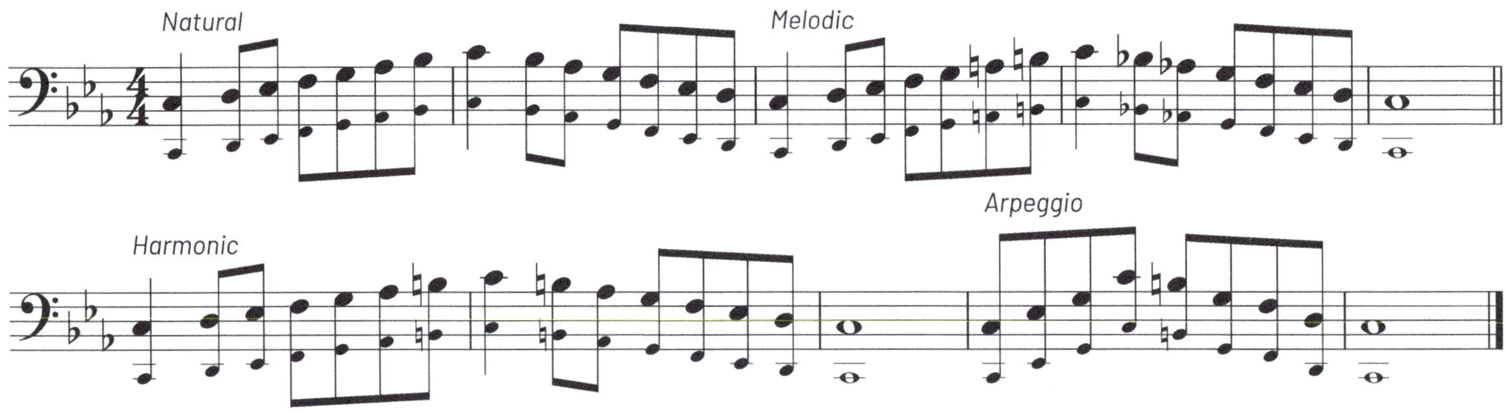

195. F MINOR SCALE

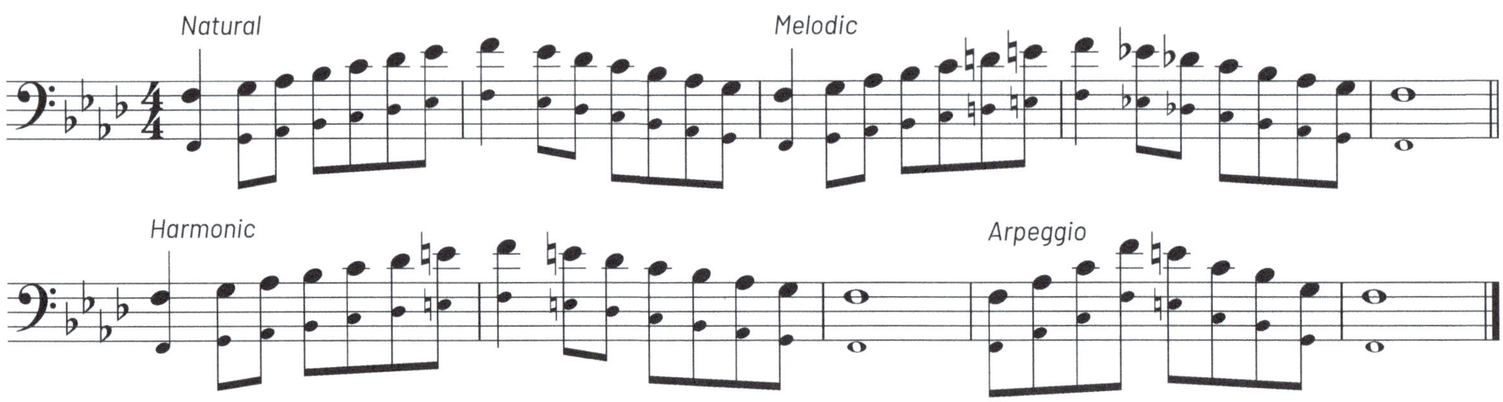

TRILL CHART

BASSOON

Here are some common trill fingerings. Trill the **red** key(s).

E♭→F

B→C♯

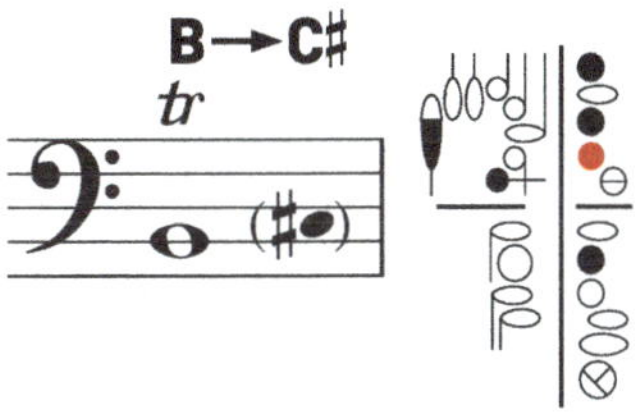

C→D♭

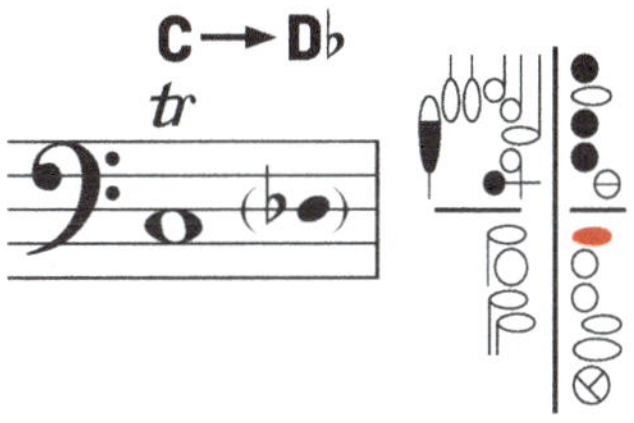

C♯→D

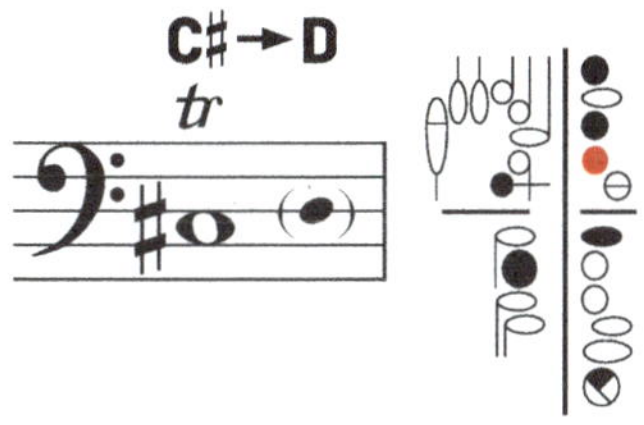

D♭→E♭

D→E♭

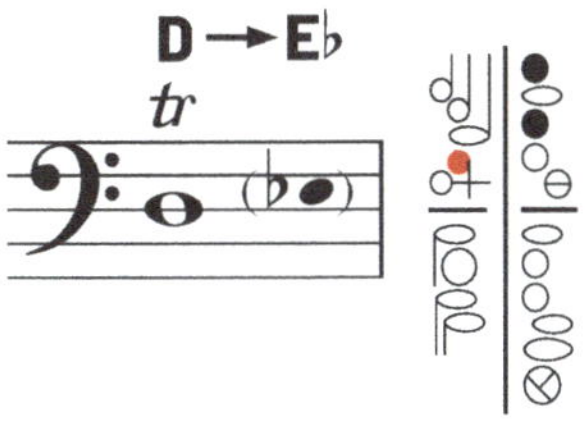

E♭→F

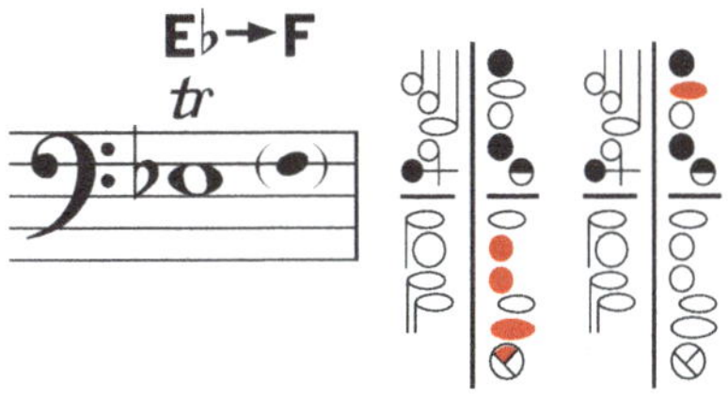

E→F♯

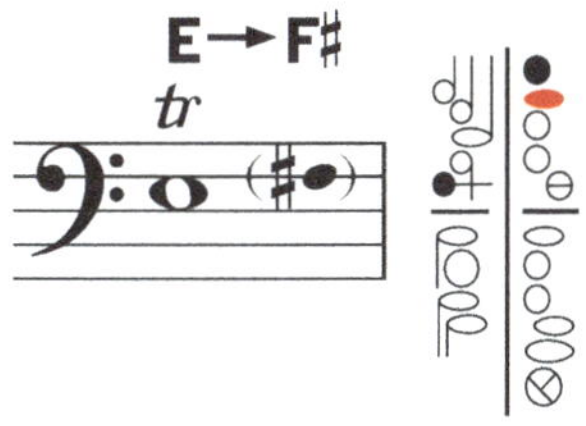

F→G

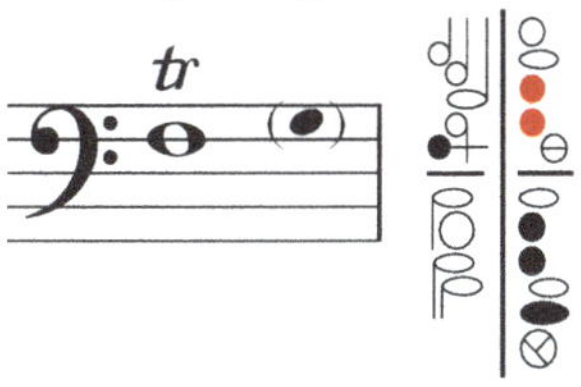

G♯→A

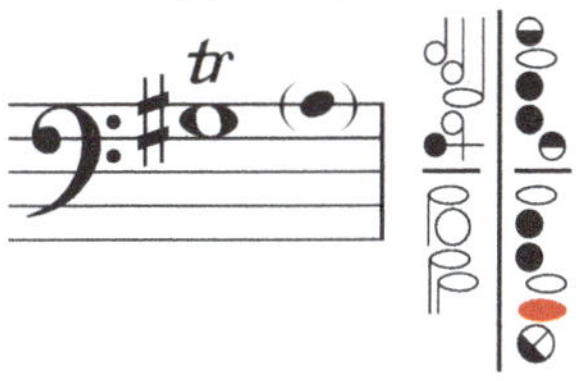

A♭→B♭

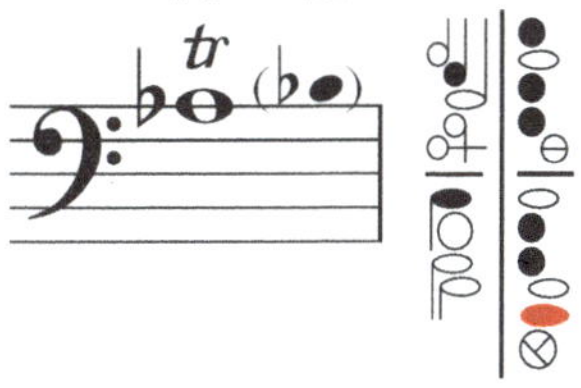

B♭→C

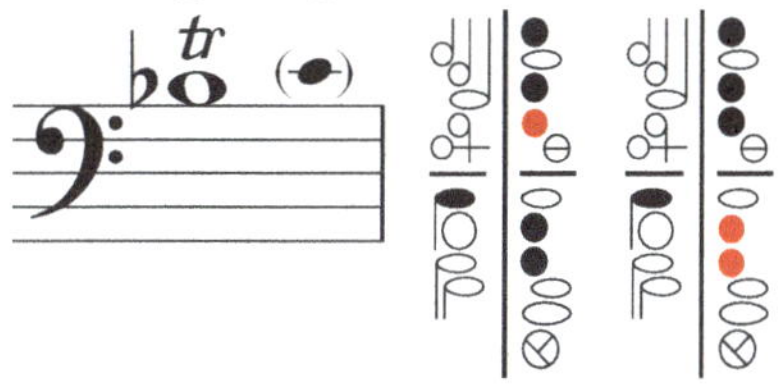

B→C♯

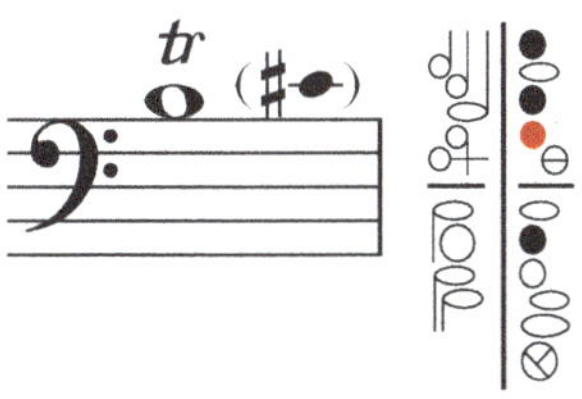

C→D♭

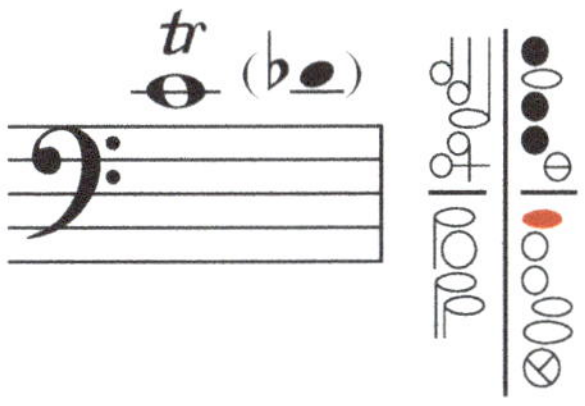

C♯→D

D→E♭

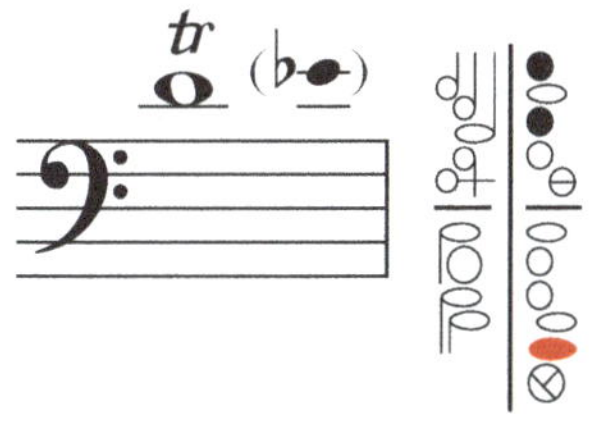

D→E

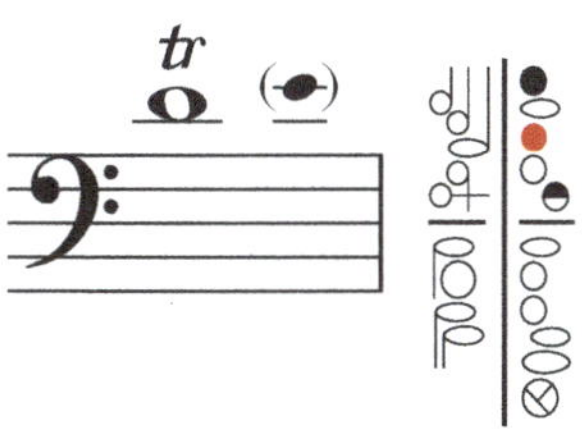

D♯→E

E♭→F

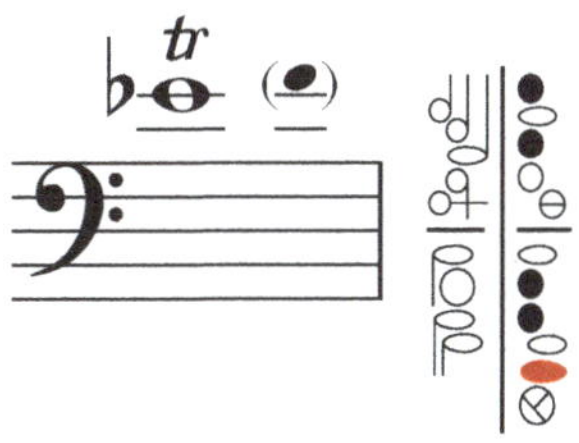

E→F

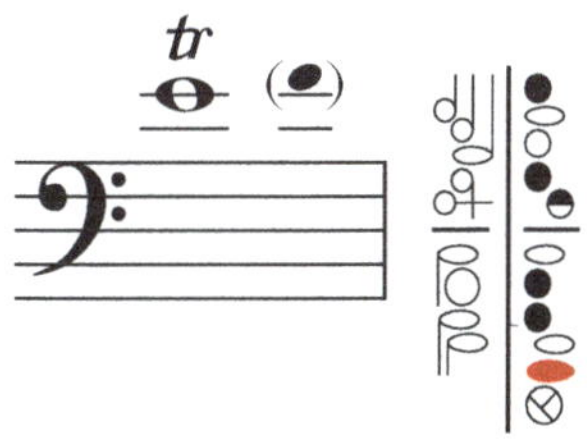

FINGERING CHART

Taking Care Of Your Instrument

Before putting your instrument back in its case after playing, do the following:

- Carefully remove the reed and blow air through it. Return to reed case.
- Remove the bocal and blow air through the larger end to remove excess moisture.
- Take the instrument apart in the reverse order of assembly. Swab out each section with a cloth swab or cleaning rod. Drop the weight of the swab through each section and pull it through. Return each section to the correct spot in the case.

○ = Open

● = Pressed down

◒ = Half hole covered

○ = Flicked

○ = Optional

The most common fingering appears first when two fingerings are shown.

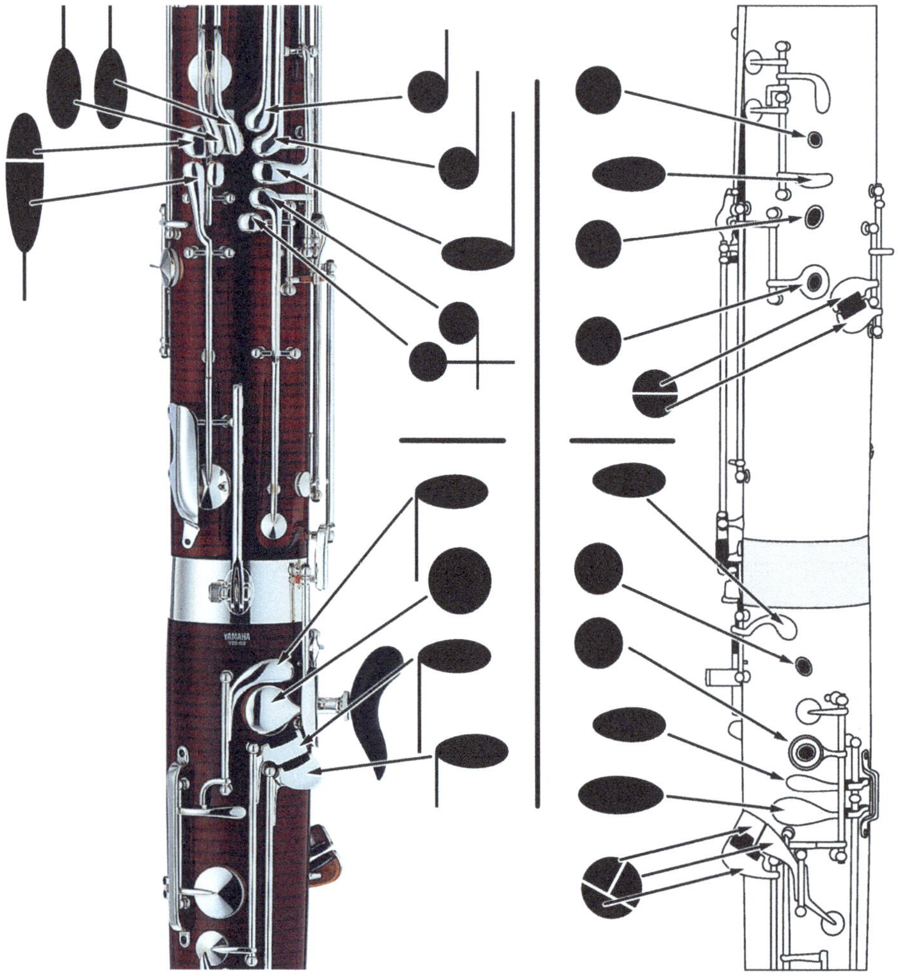

Instruments and photos courtesy of Yamaha.

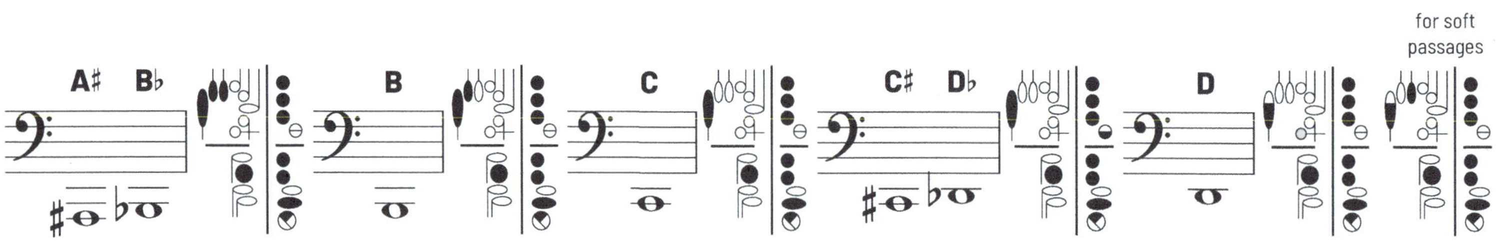

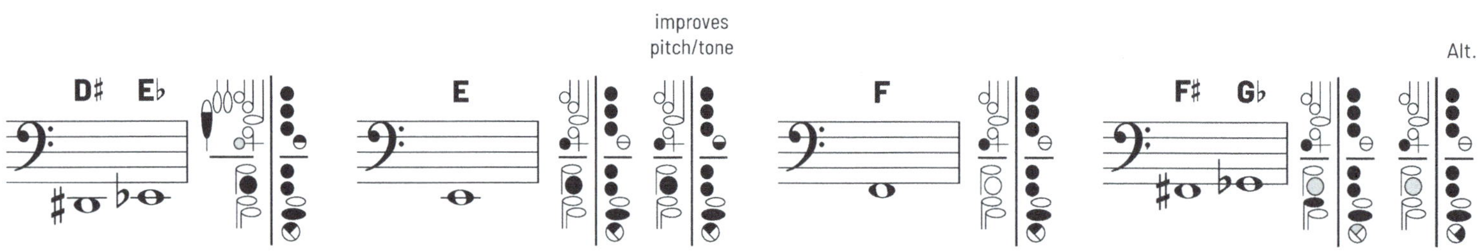

FINGERING CHART

BASSOON

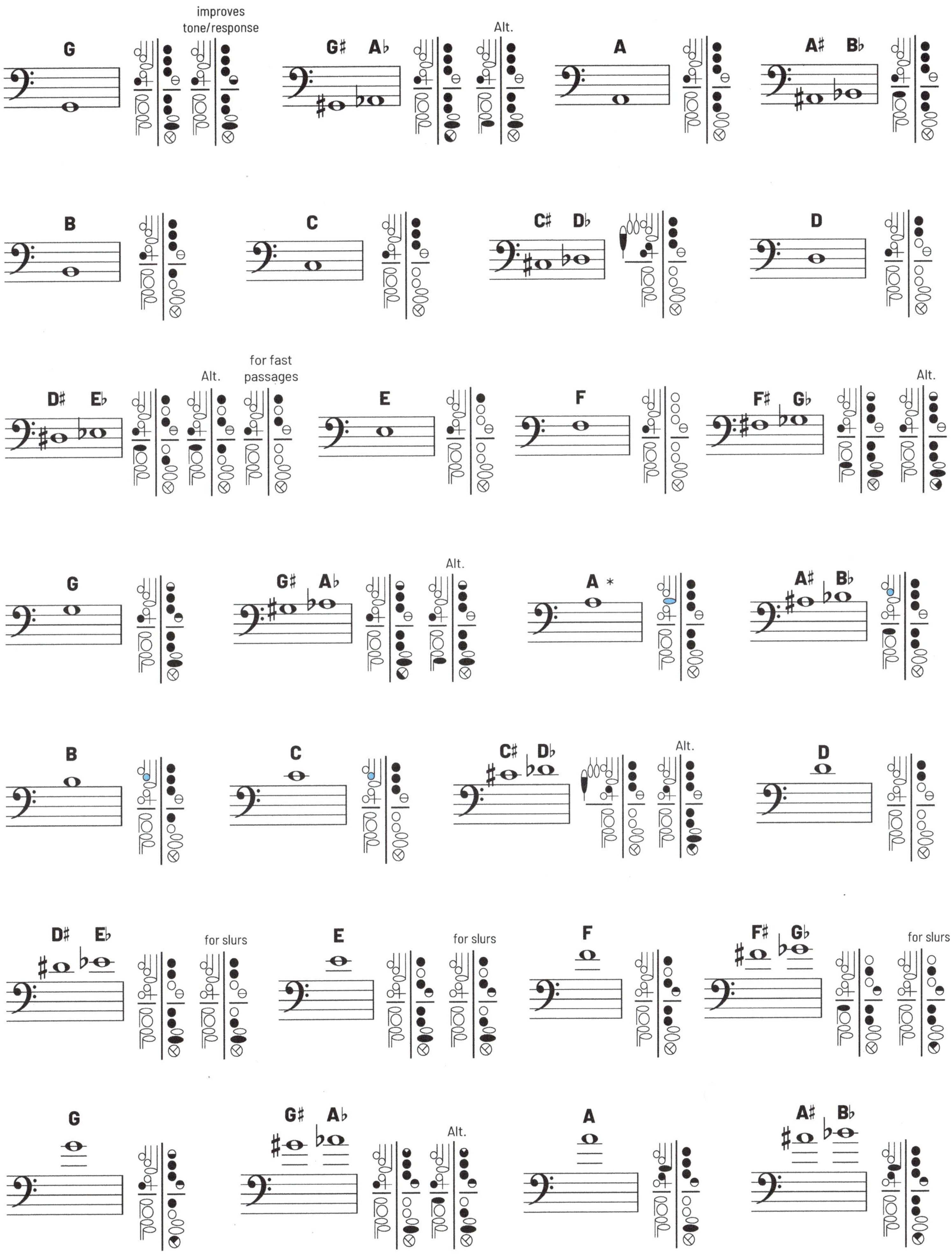

REFERENCE INDEX

Definitions (pg.)

Composers

World Music